GRAND MOVING DIORAMA OF HINDOSTAN

This edition published by Lector House in 2023

ISBN: 978-93-5800-763-3

Lector House LLP
Registered Office: H. No. 96, Block C, Tomar Colony,
Burari, Delhi – 110084, India
info@lectorhouse.com
www.lectorhouse.com

GRAND MOVING DIORAMA OF HINDOSTAN

FANNY PARKES PARLBY

2023

LECTOR HOUSE LLP

Asiatic Gallery,

BAKER STREET BAZĀR, PORTMAN SQUARE.

GRAND MOVING DIORAMA OF HINDOSTĀN,

DISPLAYING THE SCENERY OF THE HOOGLY, THE BHĀGĪRATHĪ, AND THE GANGES, FROM FORT WILLIAM, BENGAL, TO GANGOUTRĪ, IN THE HIMALAYA.

BY

فاني پارکس

* * * * *

Visitors to the Diorama are allowed to inspect

THE MUSEUM.

* * * * *

THE DIORAMA OF HINDOSTĀN

Has been Painted by
Mr. PHILIP PHILLIPS;
The FIGURES and ANIMALS by Mr. LOUIS HAGHE;
The SHIPPING by Mr. KNELL.

The whole of the Scenes of the Diorama have been arranged by Lieutenant Colonel LUARD, from his own original and unpublished sketches, taken during a residence of fourteen years in India; aided by the kindness of friends, who have placed at his disposal the original sketches of

The late Sir CHARLES D'OYLY, Bart.,
The late JAMES PRINSEP, Esq.,
The late Captain PRINSEP,
The late Colonel EDWARD SMITH,
Major WHITE,
WILLIAM PRINSEP, Esq.,
GEORGE CHINNERY, Esq.,
WELBY JACKSON, Esq.,

and the Author of "Wanderings of a Pilgrim, during Four-and-Twenty Years, in the East."

CONTENTS

LIST OF PLATES

INTRODUCTION.

In the month of October, 1589, a body of English merchants addressed a memorial to her majesty, Queen Elizabeth, requesting licence to equip three ships for the purpose of trading to the East Indies: this request appears to have been favourably received, and in 1591 the first English commercial voyage was commenced in three vessels. It proved a disastrous one; but considerable experience was obtained, and the ardour of the English merchants was but little damped by the result.

In 1599 an association of merchant adventurers was formed in London, with a capital of 30,000*l.*, for the purpose of trading *"to the East Indies and countries thereabout;"* and the royal assent was applied for and obtained to this project, *"intended for the honour of their native country, and the advancement of trade and merchandise within the realm of England."* The Charter was dated, 31st December, 1600. This association, which may be looked upon as the foundation of the present East India Company, led to a succession of voyages more or less fortunate, which, before long, resulted in the Company obtaining establishments at various places on the coast of the Peninsula, as well as among the eastern islands. The Presidencies of Madras and Bombay were first established; but that of Bengal, although the latest, was soon rendered by circumstances the most important of the three, and is now the seat of the supreme government of India.

On the 20th December, 1687, Mr. Job Charnock, the agent for the Kossimbazār factory on the Hoogly, finding it no longer safe to remain at that place, moved down to the village of Chuttanuttee, on the present site of Calcutta, with all the ships, troops, and property, where they commenced to intrench themselves. They were afterwards forced to move down the river to Ingellee, in which pestilential climate the whole force would have been carried off, had not the Emperor Aurungzebe made overtures to Mr. Charnock and allowed him to return to Chuttanuttee. In 1691 they were allowed to form a settlement there: it increased rapidly, and was permanently fixed upon as the head-quarters of the Company's establishments in Bengal.

Chuttanuttee occupied the site of the present native portion of the city; Govindpoor stood where the new Fort William is erected; and the European part of the city, including the site of the old Fort, is built within the precincts of Kalleeghatta, hence originated the modern appellation of Calcutta; and as the founder of that city, Mr. Job Charnock's name will probably be remembered as long as the British Empire in India shall exist. He died in 1692, and was buried in the old Cemetery, where his tomb is yet to be seen in the old burying-ground of St. John's Cathedral, being one of the few allowed to remain when that building was erected.

In 1695, a rebellion having broken out in Bengal, the local government applied to the Nawāb for permission to put their factories in a state of defence, and on the request not being positively refused, they hastened to erect walls of masonry, with bastions or flanking towers at the angles, round their several factories, and thus originated the fortifications of Calcutta. In 1699, Sir Charles Eyre was re-appointed to the charge of Bengal, which was then for the first time raised to the rank of a Presidency. Orders were issued that the fortifications should be strengthened and rendered regular, so as to afford a safe retreat for all their servants and property; and it was recommended to give the outline of the buildings the form of a pentagon, if possible, that being at the time considered the strongest figure of defence. In 1701–2, the court issued orders that the Fort should be made a regular pentagon with bastions, and the works be made extensive enough to accommodate all the establishments of the out-factories. In the year 1707–8, the rival interests of the "Old London" and the new "English Company" were merged into "The United Company of Merchants trading to the East Indies."

In 1742, the Mahrattas devastated the whole province, and sacked the town of Hoogly. On this occasion, the English applied for and obtained permission to dig a ditch and throw up an intrenchment round their settlement, which, if completed, would have extended more than seven miles. When little more than three miles of the ditch were completed, finding that the Mahrattas did not advance, the work was discontinued: it was, however, always known afterwards as the Mahratta Ditch; some traces of which still remain—hence the people of Calcutta are sometimes called the Ditchers.

The Nawāb Sooraj-oo-Dowlah succeeded to the government of Bengal in 1756. He entertained the greatest dislike to the English, and determined, if possible, to expel them from the country. In June, 1756, he appeared before the factory at Kossimbazār, and the place not being tenable, it surrendered. The Nawāb advanced with expedition and attacked Calcutta, which surrendered on the 20th. Mr. Holwell, with a party amounting to 146 persons, were thrown into the Black Hole—the history of which is too well known to need repetition. The Nawāb having ransacked Calcutta, changed its name to Alīnuggur, and flattering himself he had for ever extirpated the English power, thought it unnecessary to follow up the small party of refugees assembled at Fultah. In December, 1756, an armament, under the command of Colonel Robert Clive, arrived at Fultah, and recaptured Calcutta, where they found the greater part of the merchandise that had been left there, it having been reserved for the use of the Nawāb.

DIORAMA OF HINDOSTĀN.

The subject of the Diorama which we shall have the honour to explain, is the course of the Ganges from its source to Fort William, Bengal:—its picturesque scenery, the towns and temples on its banks, the religious ceremonies, and the customs of the inhabitants, both Hindū and Musalmān, will be pourtrayed. This noble river, considered the most sacred in Hindostān, takes its rise at Gangoutrī, in the Himalaya, and issues from the mountains upon the plains near Hurdwar. It passes within a few miles of Meerut, flowing on to Furrackabad, Cawnpore, and Allahabad; at the latter, it joins the Jumna, the first river of importance with which it unites. Hence its course becomes more winding, its bed wider, and the united streams flow past Mirzapūr, Chunar, Benares, and Ghazipūr. A little above Chupra, the River Ghogra falls into the Ganges on the left bank; and below Arrah, on the opposite bank, is its junction with the Soane. At Hājīpūr, the Gunduk increases the powerful stream, which flows on and passes Patna, Monghir, Bhagulpūr, Colgong, and Rajmahal, until it reaches Gopalgunj, at which place a branch of the Ganges quits the main stream, and flowing by Sooty and Moorshedabad is called the Bhāgīrathī, until it reaches Nuddea. The main stream of the Ganges running to the eastward, joins the Berhampootra, and after its union with that river, falls into the Bay of Bengal. This, the main stream of the Ganges, is not looked upon with equal veneration by the Hindūs as the branch before-mentioned, which, flowing by Sooty and Moorshedabad, is called the Bhāgīrathī, until it reaches Nuddea, at which place it is joined by the Jellinghy, and the united currents flow on, passing Calcutta, to the island of Sāgar, under the name of the Hoogly. Prior to the commencement of the nineteenth century, the Ganges had been traced by Hindū pilgrims from Hindostān into the snowy mountains that run in a direction northwest to south-east on the frontiers of India. We will now ascend the stream, stopping, as is the custom with pilgrims, at the junction of rivers, and other sacred places, considered peculiarly holy by the Hindūs, until we reach the last shrine, Gangoutrī, the source of the Holy River.

FORT WILLIAM.

Fort William, the citadel of Calcutta, is situated on the left bank of the Hoogly, about a quarter of a mile below the town; it is a European fortification, and was called Fort William in honour of his majesty King William the Third. This Citadel was commenced by Lord Clive soon after the Battle of Plassey, which was fought in 1757; it is capable of containing 15,000 men, and the works are so extensive, that 10,000 would be required to defend them efficiently. The works do not make an imposing appearance from without, nor are they perceptible until closely approached: this excites great surprise in the natives coming from the interior, who always connect the idea of great strength with great elevation. It is of octagonal form; five of the faces are regular, while the forms of the other three next the river are according to local circumstances.

The Esplanade, Chowringhee, and the site of Fort William were, so late as 1756, a complete jungle, interspersed with a few huts, and small pieces of grazing and arable land.

The view now presented shows a part of the rampart of Fort William; the Hoogly flows beneath, Calcutta appears in the distance, stretching from Chandpaul Ghāt to Chowringhee Road; the situation of the Ghāt is marked by the high chimney of the building, containing a steam engine for raising water.

The next building in the back ground is the Bank of Bengal; the long colonnade is in front of the Supreme Court of Judicature; and to the right is the Cathedral of St. John, which stands partly on the site of the old Cemetery. In clearing away the ground for its foundation, the tomb of Mr. Job Charnock, the founder of Calcutta, was discovered: he died in 1692. The tomb of Mr. Hamilton was also found, and is now placed in the same building with that of Mr. Charnock. Mr. Hamilton was surgeon to the embassy sent to the court of the Emperor Furrookhseer, and the Company are indebted to him for having induced the Emperor to grant them many privileges, and to confirm all former ones: he died in 1717. Mr. Speke was also buried in the old Cemetery, and his tomb, with those before-mentioned, is one of the few allowed to remain there on the erection of St. John's Cathedral, where they are still to be seen. The first stone of St. John's Cathedral, in Council House Street, was laid on the 6th of April, 1781. On a plate of copper, graved in the stone, is the following inscription:—"The first stone of this sacred building, raised by the liberal and voluntary subscription of British subjects and others, was laid, under the auspices of the Honourable Warren Hastings, Esq., Governor-General of India, on the 6th day of April, 1784, and the thirteenth year of his Government."

The architect was Lieutenant James Agg, of the Engineer Corps. On the 24th of June, 1787, the Church was consecrated and dedicated to St. John. Sir John Zoffani, the celebrated artist, bestowed the altar-piece, representing the Last Supper.

The Town Hall, a fine building, is rendered conspicuous by its Doric portico; it was erected by the inhabitants of Calcutta in 1804: the Government Treasury succeeds it, and in the distance is the spire of St. Andrew's Church, in the Lall Bazār.

The Government House, the principal building in Calcutta, was erected about the year 1804, during the administration of the Marquis Wellesley; the architect was Captain Wyatt, of the Engineers. The entrances, or great gateways, are each crowned by a lion, and are continually the resting-places of the *Hargīla*, the gigantic crane, commonly called the Adjutant.

The Column on the right was erected to the memory of Major-General Sir David Auchterlony, on account of his distinguished services. It is 160 feet in height, and stands on the Esplanade in front of the town.

FORT WILLIAM, BENGAL.

PRINSEP'S GHĀT.

Hargīlas or Adjutants are numerous in the Fort, and so tame, that they will allow men to pass very near them and show no signs of fear; they stalk about the Esplanade, and rest in the most picturesque manner on the highest buildings in the city.

The officer, with his bearer holding a *chatr*, or native umbrella, to protect him from the sun, is watching some monkeys; and a *griffin*, as a young cadet is called for the first year, is amusing himself with teazing one.

PRINSEP'S GHĀT.

The audience are now requested to imagine they have embarked upon the Hoogly, off Prinsep's Ghāt, the first landing-place of importance that is met with on approaching the City of Palaces. James Prinsep, Esq., died in 1840, and his fellow-citizens in Calcutta erected this ghāt to his memory, as having been one of the leaders of science in India, the promoter of every good work, a faithful and useful public servant, and a warm and true friend. The building in the distance is St. Peter's, the garrison Church in the Fort, and the vessel passing up the river is complimented by a salute from its battery. Beyond the flag-staff is the Semaphore, or telegraph, a high tower from which intelligence is conveyed by signals.

THE WATER GATE.

The Water Gate of Fort William is now before you, and the horsemen are on the Esplanade,—a road extending by the river side, from Chandpaul Ghāt, to Garden Reach. This is the favourite ride and drive, during the early morning and in the cool of the evening, of all the inhabitants of Calcutta. A *dinghī*, a native boat covered with matting, is going up the river, filled with *gharas*, or jars of coarse, red earthenware, used for holding water.

The Governor-General's pleasure boat, called the *Sona makhī*, or golden fly, is moored beyond; she has beautiful accommodations, and is perfectly suited to the river and the climate. From this point is seen the Government House: the edifice is a noble one, and particularly well adapted in its plan and interior arrangements to the climate. The external view is grand and imposing, and it is a fit and proper residence for the supreme ruler of our Indian possessions. Its two entrances or gateways are shown, and the line of houses, inhabited by Europeans, in Esplanade Row, in front of which is the Auchterlony Monument.

The long line of vessels so closely moored off the bank, are boats, called Budjerows; they are commanded by a native called a *Sarhang* or *Mānghī*, and carry 12, 14, 16, or 18 oars, and are generally used by persons going to the upper provinces.

BĀBŪ GHĀT.

This building was erected by a wealthy native gentleman, and therefore termed *Bābū* Ghāt—the title *Bābū*, given by Hindūs, is equivalent to Mr. or to Esq., and is now as common as the latter terms are among us. Numerous small boats are crowding by the steps, and a *dinghī* has just put off. A ferry boat with passengers is crossing from the opposite side of the river, in which a *chaukidār*, or native policeman, is conspicuous, with his sword and shield. The Bengālīs generally carry *chatrs* (umbrellas) during the heat of the day, made of matting, or covered with red calico.

The street now visible is Esplanade Row, which runs from Chandpaul Ghāt by the Government House to Chowringhee Road; it is full of fine houses belonging to Europeans.

CHANDPAUL GHĀT.

The people are seen crowding on Chandpaul Ghāt; and the low, semicircular building at the summit, is the Police Station. The octagonal building with its long chimney contains a steam-engine, used for raising water from the river, for the supply of the town, watering the roads, &c.; but the water used for drinking and culinary purposes, is brought from the tanks by water-carriers. It is believed that this was the first steam-engine set up in Bengal. The water passes from the engine-well into a large brick-built reservoir, and from it into aqueducts constructed on one side of the road. The Bank of Bengal is on the other side of the road called the Strand, and the high pillars of its verandahs face the Esplanade.

Colvin's Buildings appear to great advantage; they are lofty and spacious. Three merchant vessels are anchored off the Strand, and to each of their chain cables a piece of wood is attached, in a manner that prevents the water-rats from getting up them into the vessels. A native fishing-boat with her immense net fixed upon two bamboos, is making for the ghāt—perhaps bearing a freight of *Tapsi Mach*, or mango fish (so called because they come in with the mango season); hence the Hindustanī proverb, "Mangoes and fish meet of necessity." They are the great luxury of the Calcutta epicures, who make parties to Budge-budge down the river to enjoy the mango fish, as those of London resort to Blackwall for white-bait.

From the Bankshall a red boat (No. 7) is going out with a pilot to some vessel in the river. Bankshall is said to be a Dutch name for the chief landing-place, which was afterwards converted into the East India Company's marine and pilot depôt.

THE STEAM MILLS.

The fine buildings that now meet the eye are the Strand Mills, the property of the late Mr. Smithson, who erected them for the purpose of grinding corn by means of steam engines. It is said the speculation proved a failure, because the natives will not send their wheat to be ground in a mill in which it is mixed with the wheat of people of another caste, and with that sent by Europeans. It is the custom in Hindostan for each family to grind its own corn at home between two circular stones called *chakkī*, and this work is usually performed by the women. It was proposed to the King of Oude to erect steam mills for grinding corn in his dominions; but he refused to comply with the request, because it would throw the old women with their *chakkīs* out of work.

On the right is a *daunā* or donī, a country vessel, a coaster and trader, commanded by a *Sarhang*;—the crew are natives; the vessel is short, thick, clumsy, and marvellously ugly.

THE MINT.

The *Taksāl*, or Mint, a fine edifice of the Doric order, was planned and erected by Colonel Forbes, the present Mint master. The wide-ranging buildings of the new Mint, with their tall chimneys, appear to great advantage when viewed from the river. The Bengal Government set the first example of introducing extensive machinery, in the erection of the new Mint of Calcutta, which is filled with the best specimens of the skill and genius of Messrs. Watt and Co.; and the politeness of the Mint and Assay masters insures easy access to view the fine and ample machinery.

A Chinese junk on the right adds greatly to the picturesque beauty of the river, on which Arab *grabs*, and vessels from all parts of the world, are crowded together. An eye is painted on each side the bows of the Chinese junk, to enable the spirit of the vessel to see her way across the deep.

In the foreground is the hulk of a country ship under repair, beyond which are three vessels from Malacca.

BENGAL COTTAGE SCENERY.

The scene now changes to the right bank, the opposite side of the river, at sunset. On the landing-place are natives bathing, and every where the margin of the water is studded with human beings. One man is filling his *gharas* (earthen water vessels), which he carries suspended by ropes from a bamboo poised on his shoulder. Bengalī women are bringing empty water jars to fill at the river side, and in the shade a woman is returning from the holy stream on her way to some idol, bearing on her hand a brass tray containing a small vessel filled with water, and oil, and rice, and flowers for *pūjā*—that is, worship. A *Dhobī* is washing clothes by dipping them in the river, and beating them on a rough piece of slanting board, the custom of the washermen in the East.

The shop of a *Modī*, a grain merchant and seller of fruit, is now before you. Oranges, melons, limes, jackfruit, pummelos, pine-apples, all that is offered for sale in such abundance and at so small a price in this country are displayed at various seasons most invitingly. The fruit-seller is a very pious man, if we may judge from the pictures of the Hindū deities stuck on the wall of his shop, but which are too much in the shade to be very distinct. On the bamboo support of his thatch is a painting of Hūnūmān, the monkey god, in which he is represented bearing off on his shoulders the god Rām, and Sīta the beloved, from Ceylon: a fac-simile of this painting is in the Pilgrim's Museum, being one of 32 paintings of the gods purchased at the Great Fair at Allahabad for one rupee!

The natives are particularly fond of pigeons: they roost during the day on a frame-work, supported on a bamboo, as here pourtrayed; and the great delight of the pigeon-fancier is to fly his flock against that of another, making his birds wheel and turn, ascend and descend, and obey his every wish, by directing their course with a long thin bamboo. You continually see men and boys of an evening standing on the house-tops, amusing themselves with flying their pigeons.

THE FAKĪR.

THE FAKĪR.

The group in the foreground represents a *Bābū*, a native gentleman, awaiting the cool of the evening before he enters his palanquin; an attendant is supporting a *chatr*, or native umbrella, over his head, and the bearers with the palanquin are in attendance.

In front is a Muhammadan *Fakīr* leading a white bull fancifully adorned with peacocks' feathers, cowrie shells, coloured worsted tassels, bits of brightly-coloured cloth, and brass bells; the plume on the top of his neck is the tail of the *yāk*, the cow of Tartary, much used in Hindostān in the adornment of holy bulls and of horses. In the back-ground is an Hindū temple, gilded by the rays of the setting sun.

The portico or entrance to the house of an opulent *Bābū*, a Bengalī gentleman, now appears; it is of native architecture, singular and handsome; the ornaments of some of the pillars are most elaborate, and it is remarkable that each has a separate design.

THE NĀCH.

The scene now represents the interior of the building during the celebration of the festival of the *Dūrga-pūjā*, or *Dasera*, held in honour of the goddess Dūrga, and the performance of a *nāch* by the dancing-girls of Hindostān. During the *Dūrga-pūjā* holidays, which last eight or ten days, the Hindūs lay aside all kind of business, save what necessity renders indispensable to pursue, and shops and offices are shut up while that great religious ceremonial is in course of being observed.

The house, as is generally the case, is a four-sided building, having an area in the middle, on one side of which the image of the goddess is raised on a throne, and some Brahmans are in attendance. The area is open to the sky, and a temporary ceiling is formed by fastening ropes across from wall to wall, over which a cotton carpet of native manufacture, called *shatranjī*, is spread, thus forming a roof; the floor is also covered with a gay cloth of the same manufacture, and a Persian carpet.

The goddess Dūrga, in whose honour this festival is held, derives her name from the giant Dūrgŭ, whom she is represented in the act of slaying with a trident as he issues from the neck of a buffalo, whose head she has cut off. The image is that of a yellow woman with ten arms, which are stretched out and filled with instruments of war. This goddess has a thousand names, and has assumed innumerable forms.

The bright half of the month *Aswina*, the first of the Hindū lunar year, is peculiarly devoted to Dūrga. The first nine nights are allotted to her decoration; on the sixth she is awakened; on the seventh she is invited to a bower formed of the leaves of nine plants, of which the *bilwa* is the chief. The seventh, eighth, and ninth are the great days; on the last, the victims which are immolated to her honour must be killed with one blow only from a sharp sword or axe. The next day the goddess is reverently dismissed, and her image is cast into the river, which finishes the festival of the *Dasera*.

The black figure at the side of the goddess is that of Krishnŭ, one of the most popular gods of the Hindū Pantheon; he is greatly worshipped in Bengal, as well as in all parts of Hindostān, a great proportion of the Hindū population being devoted to him, and he is especially beloved by the women. A black marble figure of this popular deity stands in the Pilgrim's Museum, as well as a small brazen one of Dūrga; the latter is very ancient. Immense sums are expended by wealthy Bengalīs during the *Dūrga-pūjā*.

The *Bābū* is conversing with his European guests, and offering flowers to one of the ladies, who, seated on a sofa, is talking to those around her, and witnessing the *nāch*. The dancing-girls wear a very full petticoat of fine-coloured muslin, trimmed with deep borders of gold and silver, full satin trowsers which all but cover their naked and jewelled feet; and the *dopatta*, a large veil worn over the head, is highly embroidered. Various ornaments of native jewellery adorn their persons; their anklets are formed of numerous small brass bells that sound in time with their steps in the measured dance, and rings adorn their toes. In the thumb ring, which is about two inches in diameter, a bit of looking-glass is inserted, in which the nāch-girl often looks to see if her tresses are in order, and to adjust her flowing drapery. They dance, or rather move in a circle, attitudinizing and making the small brass bells fastened to their ankles sound in unison with their movements. Several men, the musicians of the party, attend each set of nāch-girls; they play on divers curiously-shaped native instruments.

In the hands of one of the native servants, standing near the steps, is a silver tray containing a *gulab-dānī* (a gold or silver vessel used in sprinkling rose-water on departing guests), and the smaller vessel at its side, of elegant form, contains the *'atr* of roses, which is placed on their hands at the same time.

Before the temples of Dūrga thousands of animals are annually slaughtered and offered to her image. In the portico is represented the sacrifice of a goat; the officiating Brahman, after bathing it, either in the river or in the house, puts his left hand on its forehead, marks its horns and forehead with red-lead, and repeats an invocation, in which he offers it up to the goddess thus: "O goddess, I sacrifice this goat to thee, that I may live in thy heaven to the end of ten years." He then reads an incantation in its ear, and puts flowers and sprinkles water on its head. The instrument with which the animal is to be killed is next consecrated; the goat's head is then put into an upright post, excavated at the top so as to admit the neck between its forks, the body remaining on one side the post and the head on the other; after which the executioner cuts off the head with one blow. After all the animals have been thus killed, and some of the flesh and the heads carried before the image, the officiating Brahman repeats certain prayers over these offerings and presents them to the goddess.

The square pillars of the building are of pure Hindostānī architecture, very singular, and elaborately carved.

OFFERING OF LIGHTS TO THE RIVER.

Having witnessed the *nāch* and some of the ceremonies of the *Dūrga-pūjā* festival, we now quit the illuminated area, and pass into the beautiful, the delicious moonlight of the East. Some Bengalī huts are beneath the trees; a *chaukīdar*, or native watchman, is standing before his hut, formed of straw and bamboo, on which his shield is hung; and a native beyond is cooking his evening meal.

The soft moonlight falls upon the river, and upon its bank several Bengalī women are sending off little paper boats, each containing a lamp. With what earnestness they watch these little fire-fly boats, in which they have adventured their happiness, as they float down the stream! If at the moment the paper boat disappears in the distance the lamp is still burning, the wish of the votary will be crowned with success; but, if the lamp be extinguished, the hope for which the offering was made will be doomed to disappointment. With what eagerness does the mother watch the little light, to know if her child will or will not recover from sickness! At times, the river is covered with fleets of these little lamps, hurried along by the rapid stream. Even when it is not in honour of any particular festival, natives may be seen offering lamps to Ganga (the Ganges), the sacred river.

A *patāīla* (a country vessel), and two *oolāks* are now in view; the natives always moor their vessels during the night, it being dangerous to proceed on the river during the hours of darkness.

THE MURDA GHĀT.

We now cross to the opposite side, the left bank of the Hoogly, to a *murda ghāt*, a spot where the funeral rites of the Hindūs are performed. The nearest relative, as is the custom, is stirring up the body, and pushing it into the flames with a long pole; much oil and *ghī* (clarified butter) is poured over the wood, to make it burn fiercely: in all probability the son of the deceased is performing the ceremony. We read of the Romans burning their dead, regard it in a classical light, and think of it without disgust; but when we see the ceremony really performed, it is very painful: nevertheless, a sort of absurdity is mixed with it in the mind, as "Stir him up with the long pole" flashes across the memory. On the conclusion of the ceremony, the relatives bathe and return to their homes. The *charpāī*, or native bed, on which the corpse is carried down to the river side, being reckoned unclean, is generally thrown into the stream, or left on the bank. If a large quantity of wood and *ghī* be consumed, we may imagine the deceased to have been a rich man; the relatives of the very poor scarcely do more than scorch the body, and throw it into the river, where it floats swollen and scorched—a horrible sight. The burning of the body is one of the first ceremonies the Hindūs perform for the help of the dead in a future state. If this ceremony have not been attended to, the rites for the repose of the soul cannot be performed.

Perched on the house-top are three vultures, and an *hargīla*, or adjutant, awaiting the time that they may pounce upon the remains of the corpse, when it is consigned to the holy river. These insatiate birds of prey perch upon the abutting walls, waiting their opportunity to descend; whilst others, repulsed by the attendants of the funeral fires, fly heavily across the river, passing across the native boats, through the tattered sails of which you might almost mark their flight. It is a sickening sight, rendered infinitely more sickening by the abominable effluvium which issues from the bank of death, in spite of the scented wood and other odoriferous substances, that are placed upon the funeral pile of a rich Hindū, and burnt with the body. This custom illustrates the text, "So shall they burn odours for thee." (Jeremiah xxxiv. 5.) The Hindūs believe, that persons for whom funeral rites have not been performed, wander as ghosts, and find no rest.

An English gentleman travelling *dāk* is standing on the bank; he has just crossed over, and is watching the bearers who are getting his palanquin out of the boat. *Dāk* journeys are usually performed, during the hot weather, by night, and the traveller rests at some house during the day. Of a moonlight night a *dāk* trip is far from being disagreeable.

THE PĪPAL TREE.

A Bengali village now appears beneath a group of cocoa-nut trees, beyond which the *Pīpal*-tree (ficus religiosa) is seen, with its roots exposed, the earth having been washed from them during the rains by the rising of the river. This tree is particularly venerated by the Hindūs; they believe its sacred branches to be the residence of the gods, and will never cut a branch to the injury of the tree. In front, a Hindū is sitting at worship by the side of the river; a *charpāī,* on which probably a corpse has been brought to be burned, is near the spot, also a skull and some bones: skulls are continually seen on the banks of the river.

PANHUTTĪ.

The picturesque and singular group of Bengalī temples that now open on our view are at Panhuttī—a spot well known to the English as the Grove; it is about half way between Calcutta and Barrackpore.

The Budjerow which is coming down the stream is apparently tenanted by a European gentleman; his *khidmutgar* (a servant who waits at table) is in the forepart of the vessel, and the cook-boat is astern—the sails of the latter in the torn and worn-out state in which they are so continually seen.

THE WELL, AND PALM TREES.

The bamboo stage is erected for the purpose of watering the land. The river water is collected in a deep pool, between two brick walls, across which a small stage is fixed, on which a man stands, and his business is to empty the leathern skin which comes up full of water into the reservoir above, prepared for its reception. A long bamboo, with a large weight of earth attached to it at one end, is poised on a stage above, on which a native stands and causes the end towards the river to sink by the weight of his foot; when the skin below, which is attached to a thin bamboo from above, is filled with water, he removes his foot, which causes the water-bag to rise to the height of the reservoir, when the man below empties it and lets it fall again. In some parts, instead of a skin, a basket is used, which is rendered waterproof inside by a coating of clay and mud. Water is thus conveyed to a very great distance from the banks of a river. The fields in India are irrigated with as much care as is bestowed upon a garden, and three harvests are often obtained.

The Bengalī *jantŭ* for watering the land happily illustrates this passage of Scripture, "Where thou sowedst thy seed, and wateredst it with thy foot, as a garden of herbs." (Deut. xi. 10.)

The palm trees next to the well are remarkably beautiful; they are portraits. The one displaying the broad leaves is the fan-palm, from which the large *pankhas* are made—one leaf alone forms the *pankha,* or fan, of which three specimens are to be seen in the Museum.

THE RATHJATTRA.

The scene represents the *Rathjattra,* or festival of the chariot, as it took place near Serampore, on the right bank of the Hoogly; and in this manner the ceremonies are performed in innumerable towns and villages in Hindostān; but the place most celebrated for this worship is the Temple of Jaganāth, in Orissa. In the scene representing a *nāch,* in the house of a Bengalī *bābū,* you beheld the figure of "Krishnŭ the Beloved" playing on a flute, standing by the side of the goddess Dūrga. At the *Rathjattra,* Krishnŭ is worshipped as *Jaganāth* or lord of the universe. In some period of Hindū history he was accidentally killed by a hunter, who left the body to rot under a tree where it fell. Some pious person, however, collected the bones of Krishnŭ, and placed them in a box, where they remained: a king who was performing religious austerities, to obtain some favour of Vishnū, was directed by the latter to form the image of Jaganāth and put inside these bones of Krishnŭ, by which means he should obtain the fruit of his religious austerities. The king inquired who should make this image, and was commanded to pray to Vishnŭ-Kŭrmŭ, the architect of the gods. He did so, and obtained his request; but the architect at the same time declared, that if any one disturbed him while preparing the image, he would leave it in an unfinished state. He then began, and in one night built a temple upon the blue mountain in Orissa, and proceeded to prepare the image in the temple; but the impatient king, after waiting fifteen days, went to the spot; on which the architect of the gods desisted from his work, and left the image without hands or feet. The king was very much disconcerted; but on praying to Brŭmha, he promised to make the image famous in its present shape. The king now invited all the gods to be present at the setting up of this image: Brŭmha himself acted as high priest, and gave eyes and soul to the god, which completely established the fame of Jaganāth. In the Museum is a small fac-simile of this god, which was brought from Pooree, in Orissa; and at its side is the seal with which the Brahmans stamp the worshippers on the breast and arms, and also a figure in black marble of Krishnŭ, highly ornamented. The height of the *ruth,* or chariot, is forty-two feet, supported on sixteen wheels, and the horses in front are of wood. Ropes are attached to the bars below; and the car, with the monstrous idol within it, is drawn by thousands of frantic devotees. Looking out from the top is seen the head of Jaganāth. The Brahmans adorn him during the festivals with silver or golden hands—an offering of a pair of golden ones is considered an act of great devotion.

One of the Hindū poets, in answer to the question, "Why has Vishnŭ assumed a wooden shape?" (alluding to the image of Jaganāth) says, "The troubles of his family have turned Vishnŭ into wood: in the first place, he has two wives, one of whom (the goddess of learning) is constantly talking, and the other (the goddess of prosperity) never remains in one place: to increase his troubles, he sits on a snake, his dwelling is in the water, and he rides on a bird." All the Hindūs acknowledge it is a great misfortune for a man to have two wives, especially if both live in one house.

After many ceremonies have been performed, the god is drawn forth in his car, and at the expiration of eight days he is conveyed back to the place whence he came. The natives dance before the car, and the procession is accompanied with drums, tom-toms, horns, and all sorts of discordant native music.

Dancing is considered a religious ceremony among the Hindūs. The Brahmans consider it an act of devotion to the god.

WATER CARRIERS.

The natives of India carry water long distances in a couple of leathern bags prepared for the purpose and hung across a bullock; the *behishtī*, or water-carrier, by the side of the stream, is filling the skins from his *mashk*, or water-bag, and another man is bringing up his leathern bag for the same purpose.

An Hindū girl is taking down a large net to the fisherman in the river, where he has just spread his own net. On the top of his head a small basket is fixed, into which he puts whatever he may catch; and floating on the water, attached to his waist by a long string, is a *gharā*, an earthen vessel, also used as a depository for the fish.

The *oolāk* is floating timber to Calcutta, secured to her by ropes over the side. She is ornamented by a border of impressions of the human hand in white paint on the side of the stern, and has also an eye painted on each side of her bows; which the Hindūs, like the Chinese, consider necessary, to enable the spirit of the vessel to see its way upon the waters.

BARRACKPORE.

We now cross the Hoogly to Barrackpore, called by the natives *Achánuck*, corrupted from Charnock, the founder of Calcutta, who lived here. In the park is the country-house of the Governor-General; and the military cantonment affords accommodation to six regiments of native infantry. There is nothing remarkable about the Government House; it is a plain edifice of one story in height, with lofty rooms; the aviary, the menagerie, the garden, and a pleasant promenade, where the society of the station assemble, are the most attractive features of the place. The regiments here, with the Artillery at Dum-Dum (seven miles from Calcutta), and the troops in Fort William, constitute the presidency division of the army, which is commanded by a general officer, who resides at Barrackpore.

BARRACKPORE.

The Governor-General having come up the river in his yacht, the *Sona-makhī*, towed by a steamer, is represented as quitting the vessel to land at Barrackpore. The troops are drawn out awaiting his arrival; the elephants are ready to convey him to the house; the aid-de-camps are in attendance; and each of their horses is held by a *sāīs*, or groom, who carries in his hand a *chaurī*, to keep flies from the animal.

In the back-ground is a *shutur-sawār*, a man armed, and mounted on a camel, for the purpose of carrying messages express. This animal, of a much lighter description than the camel of burthen, can trot exceedingly fast, and will go from sixty to eighty miles a day, without distress: the pace is very rough, and the riders are not considered long lived. The camel's neck is ornamented with small brass bells—a common appendage to couriers in many countries: it is also adorned with blue beads, cowrie shells, and gaily-coloured cloth and tassels: a small piece of wood is inserted in the animal's nostrils, to which is attached a thin cord, by which it is guided.

The Mausoleum in the Park, of the Corinthian order, to the left of the Government House, was erected by Lord Minto, at his own cost, to commemorate the names of the officers who fell at Java and the Mauritius.

THE TRAVELLER'S PALM.

Some cows and a buffalo are beneath a *pīpal* tree in the park. On the bank is the *sarput*, or *sirkī*, high jungle-grass that often rises to the height of sixteen feet; the bloom waves gracefully, bending to the wind, and elegantly recovers its position.

The next is the castor-oil plant (ricinus communis), much cultivated in Bengal; the oil extracted from the seeds being used medicinally, as well as for burning in lamps.

The tree with the broad and singular leaves is called the Traveller's Palm: if a knife is stuck into the stem a pure water gushes out. It grows in the most sandy tracts where no water is to be found; hence it is called the Traveller's Palm. Dr. Wallich mentioned this circumstance, and at the same time he struck his knife into the tree, of which the one before you is a portrait.

The cart is the common *hackerī* of the country, and the natives belonging to it are asleep beneath it; a *chadda*, or cloth, is drawn over their heads to protect them from the musquitoes, and their slippers are laid on one side.

The Muhammadan Fakīr, a religious mendicant, in front of the group, is a picturesque personage; he wanders over the country, and supports himself on alms.

PLASSEY.

The high walls of the Nawāb's hunting-house at Plassey are now before you, and we cannot but regard the spot with feelings of the deepest interest, as it is the house in which Colonel, afterwards Lord Clive rested for a short time during the engagement. The famous battle of Plassey, which may be said to have decided the fate of India, was fought on the 23rd June, 1757, on the plains of Plassey, about thirty miles south of Moorshedabad; near the spot selected for the Nawāb Sooraj-oo-Dowlah's entrenched camp, the river at that period made a remarkable bend, in shape like a horse-shoe. In a mango *top*, or grove, a little more than a mile from the enemy, Colonel Clive had taken up his position: the trees were planted in regular rows, as is usual in the country, and all around the *top* was a bank of earth, which afforded a good breast-work for the troops, and also a ditch beyond. One detachment was stationed at Plassey House, which was made use of by Colonel Clive during the conflict. About eight o'clock A.M. the battle commenced; and at eleven, Colonel Clive held a conference with his officers at the drum-head, when it was decided to maintain the cannonade during the day, and at midnight to make an attack on the Nawāb's camp. The fate of Sooraj-oo-Dowlah was sealed by his flight towards the capital, mounted on a fleet *sawārī* camel, accompanied by about 2000 horsemen. By five o'clock the English had taken possession of the whole intrenchment and camp, with no other obstacle than was presented by the enormous mass of baggage, stores, camp-equipage, and cattle, scattered around them.

The lofty stage of bamboos in the field is erected sufficiently high to be a refuge from wild beasts; it is thatched, and the native farmer places a servant there to keep watch, especially during the night, at the time the corn is nearly ripe. When a buffalo, or wild hog, comes into the field, the keeper takes a wisp of lighted straw in one hand, and in the other a dried skin containing broken bricks, pots, &c., bound up on all sides; and in this manner he approaches the animal, shaking his lighted straw and making a loud noise, on which it immediately runs away. "The boar out of the wood doth waste it, and the wild beast of the field doth devour it." (Psalm lxxx. 13.) The wild hogs and buffaloes make great havoc in the fields of the Hindūs.

Below the stage is a domestic buffalo and a group of Bengalī cows. The buffalo is a very useful beast of burthen, yields a rich but strong milk, which is generally made into *ghī* (clarified butter). This animal has no hump—a fact not universally known by those who have not visited India; on the contrary, the buffalo is generally supposed to have the hump. Those sold under the denomination of buffalo humps are from the common bull or cow of Hindostan.

THE ELEPHANT ESTABLISHMENT.

Not far distant from Plassey is the Company's *Fīl-khana*, or Elephant establishment, whence the animals are coming down to the side of the river. One of the elephants in the distance is raising his *mahout*, or driver, with his trunk, to enable him to gain his seat on his neck: another is drinking, taking up the water with his proboscis and pouring it into his own mouth; a third is lying in the river enjoying the coolness, whilst his attendants are scrubbing and cleaning him.

A group of natives, attendants on the elephants, are sitting round a fire, baking the large cakes that form the repast of these animals, added to a small dinner of half a *pīpul-tree*, or a hundred-weight of grass! A *mahout*, or driver, is very fond of whispering to his elephant some superstitious tale; which, if the animal does not understand, it is amongst the few things this most wonderful of God's creatures does not comprehend.

THE ELEPHANT ESTABLISHMENT.

MOSQUE NEAR MOORSHEDABAD.

A beautiful *Masjid*, or Mosque (a Muhammadan place of worship), which is on the bank forms a picturesque object; beyond which is a *ghāt* and some houses, near Moorshedabad, as also a long range of buildings, belonging to the palace of the Nawāb.

MOORSHEDABAD—THE PALACE.

Moorshedabad became the seat of the Bengal Government A.D. 1704. It was transferred to this place from Dacca, by the Nawāb Jaffier Khan, who was appointed Soubadar of Bengal by Aurungzebe. The City of Moorshedabad continued to be the seat of the British Government until A.D. 1771, when it was transferred to Calcutta. During the reign of Aliverdi Khan, a palace was erected at Moorshedabad, which was ornamented with pillars of black marble, brought from the ruins of Gour; this building is still in existence. The new palace of the Nawāb erected by the government, is a magnificent edifice, and reflects the highest honour on the architect, General Macleod, C.B.: it was commenced in the time of Humaioon Jah, the late *nizām*, who died in 1838, and was succeeded by his son, the present Nawāb. This splendid building, which is in the European style, and of dazzling whiteness, is a beautiful object from the river, of which it commands a fine prospect, rendered peculiarly interesting by the variety and elegance of the native vessels, so numerous at this station.

The *Mor-pankhī*, as the Nawāb's state-barge is called, is used during certain festivals at Moorshedabad: boats of this description are numerous, and of different forms, some towering very high, displaying all the colours of the peacock, and all are brilliantly painted and highly gilt. A band of native musicians follow the state-barge in another tastefully-decorated boat, and the scene on the river during the festival is highly picturesque.

Here also are seen the snake-boats: they shoot past you with great swiftness when rowed by twenty men, from their amazing length and extreme narrowness.

Through the influence of Mr. Hamilton, surgeon to the Embassy sent by the local government to the Emperor Furrookhseer, in the year 1713, the use of the Mint at Moorshedabad was placed at the disposal of the Government of India.

The great object of dread to the Nawāb Sooraj-oo-Dowlah, in 1757, was the fire of the English vessels of war, of the effects of whose broadsides he had received exaggerated accounts; and, in the excess of his timidity, he conceived it possible that they might proceed up the great branch of the Ganges, and then come down the Kossimbazar river to Moorshedabad; to guard against which, he caused large piles to be sunk across that stream, opposite to Sooty, about twenty miles above the city. A toll is now levied at Jungipūr for keeping open the entrance of the Bhagirathī, as this branch of the Ganges is called.

THE WRECK.

The scene now opens on the right bank of the Ganges. We quitted the Bhagruttī (a branch of the sacred river) at Sooty, and have now entered upon the main stream, at a point where it is of amazing breadth, the view of it only terminating with the horizon: the waves roar, and roll, and foam like those at sea; whilst a *tūfān* (one of the heavy storms of India) is blowing fiercely, accompanied by thunder, lightning, heavy rain, and utter darkness. The impetuous stream, rushing with the force of a torrent, undermines the banks of the river, and tears up forest trees by their roots. A voyage at this time is particularly dangerous; native vessels are swept along with amazing velocity, and when a *tūfān* is encountered, like the one now blowing, they are frequently wrecked.

Three *dāndīs* (native boatmen) have been swept by the violence of the waves from the mast of their sinking vessel; they are striving to regain their hold: the rest of the crew have sunk to rise no more. These men are admirable swimmers; they may possibly be carried along by the current and rescued on some turn of the river, unless from the violence of the storm they are carried out into the middle of the stream, and swept onwards, until, overcome by exhaustion, they sink beneath the waves.

During some periods of the year, a voyage on the Ganges is attended with great risk. The natives quote the Persian saying as a consolation under misfortune, "'What is the use of taking precautions, since what has been ordained must happen.' Truly saith the proverb, 'If the diver were to think of the jaws of the crocodile, he would never gather precious pearls.'"

A TŪFĀN.

The Budjerow is taking in her sails; and the *sahib*, or gentleman on board, is likely to go without his dinner, as his cook-boat, with her torn sails, will most likely be unable to come alongside, and hand it over to the servants.

A voyage up the Ganges may be performed in boats, as various in shape as in size: a Pinnace is a first-class vessel; the next is a Budjerow, which draws very little water, and is divided into two commodious rooms, which may be furnished according to the taste of the traveller: a complete establishment consists of a horse-boat, a washerman's-boat, and a cook-boat; in this country the cooking is always performed in a separate vessel.

The *dinghī*, or wherry, now making for the land, is generally manned by two rowers and a steersman: these boats are of slight construction, with a circular awning of bamboo-work and matting, under which a person can sit, and though in general well managed, are by no means to be considered safe conveyances.

RAJMAHAL.

The ruins of the palace of Rajmahal are on the bank. During the reign of Akbar, about 1591, Raja Maun Singh fixed upon this city as the capital of Bengal, and changed its name to Raja-Mahul—the Raja erected the palace, and surrounded the town with a rampart of brick and other fortifications. In 1608, the seat of government was removed hence to Dacca, by Islam Khan; but in 1639, the Sultan Shah Shuja brought it back again, and strengthened the fortifications, of which, however, few traces are now to be seen.

Prior to 1638 this town was the residence of the Sultan Shah Shuja, the brother of Aurunzebe; but few vestiges of its ancient magnificence now remain. The ruins of his palace are still standing, but have been much injured by the encroachments of the Ganges. Cows now ruminate quietly beneath the black marble arches that overlook the river, or seek for shelter in its empty halls, which still present images of their former grandeur. The marble floor of the Mosque remains, and a fine old *bāolī* (a large well). Around Rajmahal is a beautiful *jangal* of magnificent bamboos, fine clumps interspersed with date-palm trees overshadowing the cottages, around which are a number of small cows and fowls of a remarkably good breed: every thing has an air of comfort, and the walks in all directions are cool and pleasant. The steamers from Calcutta take in their coal a mile below, and therefore do not destroy the beauty of the old ruins with their smoke, and noise, and Birmingham appearance. The Rajmahal hills are distant about five miles inland.

Sooraj-oo-Dowlah, after his flight from Plassey, reached Rajmahal, and took shelter in the buildings of a deserted garden, where he was discovered by a *Fakīr* named Dana Shah, whose nose and ears he had ordered to be cut off thirteen months before. This man recognized him, made the circumstance known, and the Nawāb was carried a prisoner back to Moorshedabad, where he was murdered by order of Meerun, the son of the new Nawāb Meer Jaffier Khan. His mangled remains were placed on an elephant, exposed throughout the city, and finally interred. Thus perished Sooraj-oo-Dowlah, in the twentieth year of his age, and the fifteenth month of his reign; a prince whose short career was connected in a most important manner with the British interests in India, both for good and evil.

SĪCKRĪ-GALĪ.

A country vessel is being towed by her crew round a rocky point; each man has his own *gūn*, or track-rope, fastened to a short, thick piece of bamboo, which he carries over his shoulder. A Pinnace, or budjerow, tracks, with ten or twelve men, upon one rope only.

The Sīckrī-galī pass, during the Hindū and Muhammadan Governments, was the commanding entrance from Bahar into Bengal, and was fortified with a strong wall; however, in 1742, a Mahratta army of cavalry passed into Bengal through the hills above Colgong. The village of Sīckrī-galī is eighteen miles above Rajmahal at the base of a high rocky eminence, commanding a fine view of two ranges of hills. There is here the tomb of a celebrated Muhammadan Saint, Pīr Pointī, and a cave in limestone rock; and higher up, at a place called Pīr Pointī, now a mass of ruins, is another tomb of the saint.

This pass is close upon the Rajmahal hills, and the only European inhabitant lives in the *Bangla*, commonly called Bungalow, the house at the foot of the hill. Wild beasts sometimes come to this place at night, and the footmarks of the tiger are often to be seen in the garden. Jackals roam howling through the village; bears, tigers, rhinoceroses, leopards, hogs, deer of all kinds, abound here, and feathered game in the hills. Elephants are absolutely necessary to enable a man to enjoy shooting amidst the high grass and thorny thickets. The place is so much disturbed by the people who go into the hills for wood, that the game retreat farther into the *jangal*. When a gentleman goes out shooting on foot, the *dandīs* accompany him with long poles, to beat the bushes. In the marshy plains under the hills of this pass good shooting is to be found, but on account of tigers it is dangerous.

SĪCKRĪ-GALĪ.

THE RAJMAHAL HILLS.

Beyond the heavy rain which is pouring down, the hills of Rajmahal are seen in the distance; they are beautifully wooded, and full of game of every description. No scenes can be more picturesque than those in the interior. The wild climbers hang from the forest trees in luxuriant beauty, especially that magnificent one, the *cachnar* (bauhinia scandens)—a specimen of its leaves gathered in these hills is in the Museum.

The *dandīs* from the boats that anchor at Sīckrī-galī go up the hills in gangs to cut wood for firing, and bring it down in great quantities.

The *byā* birds hang their long nests from the extreme end of the slight branches of the delicate *bābul*-tree pendant over a pool or stream for security. The Museum also contains nests of this little bird suspended on the broad leaf of the fan-palm. The fable declares that the "Old birds put a fire-fly into their nests every night to act as a lamp." For a further account of these interesting little creatures, see "Wanderings of a Pilgrim," (vol. I. 220, 221, and vol. II. 74). The marshes at the foot of the hills are full of leeches the low-lands abound with wild fowl, hares, and partridges of a peculiar sort, said to be found only at Rajmahal, and one other station in India.

The hill-men are a most singular race of people; they are about five feet high, very active, remarkable for lightness and suppleness of limb, with the piercing and restless eye, said to be peculiar to savages. They wear their hair drawn tight up in a knot on the very top of their head, the ends fastened in with a wooden comb. They are good-natured, gay-looking people. Their principal food is Indian corn, boiled and mashed. They kill wild hogs with a poisoned arrow, taking the precaution to cut out the flesh around the wound before they eat the animal. Their bows and arrows are rough and wild-looking; the strips of feather on the latter are from the wing of the vulture. They assert that they procure the poison, into which they dip their arrows, from a remote hill-tribe, and are ignorant of its nature: it appears to be a carefully guarded secret. Three of these arrows are in the Museum. At the proper season the hill-men descend into the plains to gather in the crops of uncut rice.

A country boat filled with bales of cotton is floating down the stream; and the crew of a Dacca *oolāk*, which is aground, are striving to shove her into deeper water.

A native, sitting on the bank, is quietly watching the noisy scene, and smoking his *nāriyal*, or cocoa-nut pipe, by the side of his *charpāī*, or bed, which is on the bank. Native vessels are towed by the *dāndīs*, or boatmen, most part of the way, except during the rains. These men work from daylight till sunset in the most laborious way, frequently in the water for hours, up to their middles, towing the vessel or shoving it with their backs over sand banks: their labour does not cease until the boats are *lugāo'd* (moored) at night; then they cook on shore and eat their daily meal of boiled rice and curry, or flour cakes, called *chappatīs*. Occasionally, when a fair wind blows, they get some rest; for then an immense square sail is hoisted, tacks, sheets, and haul-yards are fast belayed: they all go to sleep except the steersman, and the safety of the boat depends upon the rotten state of the cordage and sails: frequently very strong and sudden squalls come on, and, before a single rope is let go, every thing is blown to ribbons.

THE FOOLISH FAKĪR.

Beneath a group of beautiful palm-trees, a half-witted young *Fakīr*, adorned with peacocks' feathers, is sitting and talking to the men around him, who regard as prophetic whatever his wandering and unsettled mind induces him to utter, and look upon him as the favourite of heaven—the natives treat persons thus afflicted with the greatest kindness, and supply them with food. A leaf of the fan palm, here represented, may be seen in the Museum. The whole group, as well as the trees, are portraits.

On the sands below and close to the edge of the river, is an Hindū in the last stage of illness. His friends have carried him down to the sacred stream on a *charpāī*, (a rude native bed,) and are in the act of making him drink the Ganges water, ere they half immerse his body in the sacred stream. His wife, on the edge of the bed, is weeping, and her *dopatta* (or veil), is drawn over her face; the Brahman is offering the prayers usual on this occasion.

The Hindūs are extremely anxious to die in sight of the Ganges, that their sins may be washed away in their last moments. A person in his last agonies is frequently carried on his bed, by his friends or relatives, in the coldest or in the hottest weather, from whatever distance, to the river-side, where he lies, if a poor man, without a covering day and night, until he expires. With the pains of death upon him, he is placed up to the middle in water and drenched with it; leaves of the shrub goddess, the sacred *tulsī* plant, are also put into his mouth, the marks on the pebble god, the *Salagram* are shown to him, and his relations call upon him to repeat, and repeat for him, the names of Rām, Hurī, Ganga, &c. In some cases the family priest repeats some prayers, and makes an offering to Voitŭrŭnēē, the river over which, they say, the soul is ferried, after leaving the body. The relations of the dying man spread the sediment of the river on his forehead and breast, and afterwards with the finger write on this sediment the name of some deity. If a person should die in his house, and not by the river-side, it is considered as a great misfortune, as he thereby loses the help of the goddess in his last moments. If a person choose to die at home, his memory becomes infamous.

If these unfortunate people recover, after having been exposed by their relatives to die on the banks of the river, they take refuge in the village of Chagdah on the left bank of the Matabangah, forty-six miles from Calcutta, of which people who ought to be *corpses*, are the sole inhabitants. They are considered to prefer a debased existence to a righteous end, agreeing therein with the highest authorities. Pope's Homer makes Achilles in the Elysian fields say:—

"Rather I'd choose laboriously to bear
A weight of woes, and breathe the vital air,
A slave to some poor hind that toils for bread,
Than reign the scepter'd monarch of the dead."

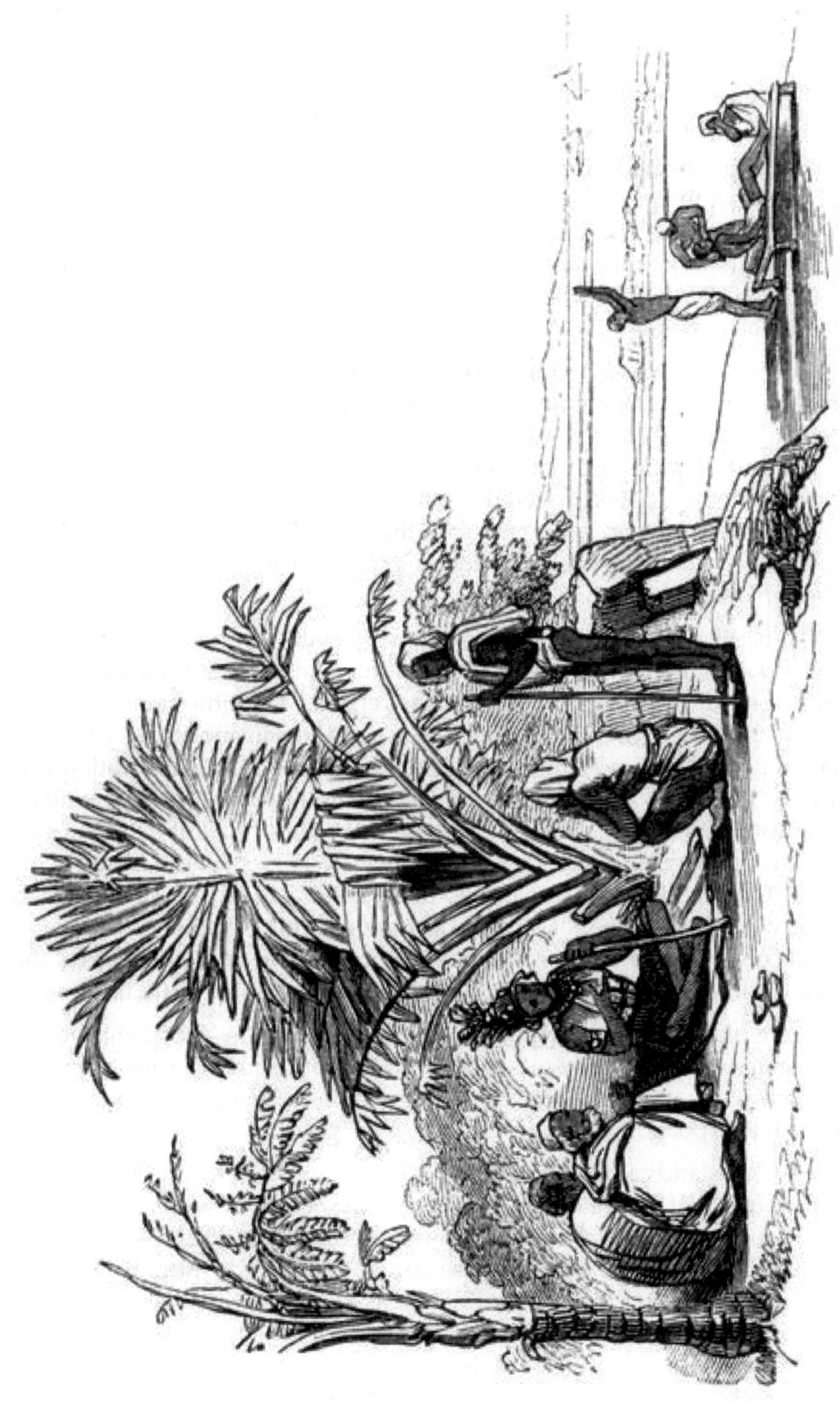

THE FOOLISH FAKĪR.

Solomon deems it better to be a live dog than a dead lion; and Job, called by Byron "the Respectable," says, "Why should a living man complain?" to which Byron adds, "For no other reason that I can see, except that a dead man cannot." In the face of these grave authorities the Hindostanī proverb is of a different opinion, which asserts "it is better to die with honour, than live with infamy."

The passage in the Psalms, "They shall be a portion for foxes," appears obscure; but give it the probable rendering, "they shall be a portion for jackals;" and then the anathema becomes plain and striking to an Hindū, in whose country the disgusting sight of jackals, devouring human bodies, may be seen every day. The dying who are left by the side of the Ganges, are sometimes devoured alive by these animals in the night.

Lugāo'd, or moored off a sand-bank, is a budjerow, her baggage, and her cook-boat. The crews are cooking and eating their dinners on the sand-bank, and will not recommence their voyage until daybreak, the river being too dangerous to allow of their proceeding further during the hours of darkness. On a clean dry bank in the centre of the Ganges, covered with the finest and most sparkling sand, it is far more agreeable to *lugāo* your vessel for the night, than on the banks of the river: it is cooler, and you are better defended against thieves; nevertheless a look-out must be kept during the night.

"Shall be likened unto a foolish man, which built his house upon the sand," &c., (Matt. vii. 26.) The fishermen in Bengal build their huts in the dry season on the beds of sand, from which the river has retired. When the rains set in, which they often do very suddenly, accompanied with violent north-west winds, and the waters pour down in torrents from the mountains, a fine illustration is given of our Lord's parable: "the rains descended, the floods came, and the winds blew, and beat upon that house, and it fell." In one night multitudes of these huts are frequently swept away, and the place where they stood is, the next morning, undiscoverable. On one of these occasions a Hindū child was carried down the stream, seated on a part of the roof of a hut, and rescued from destruction at Allahabad. The child could not tell whence she had been carried away by the force of the torrent, nor could the little creature remember the names of her parents.

In some parts of Bengal, whole villages are every now and then swept away by the Ganges when it changes its course. This river frequently runs over districts, from which, a few years before, it was several miles distant. "A nation whose land the rivers have spoiled." (Isa. xvii. 2.)

The rocky islands of Colgong in the distance are singular and beautiful, there are four of them, of unequal size. Rocks on rocks, covered with fine foliage, they rise in the centre of the river which runs like a mill-sluice, and is extremely broad. They say that no one lives upon these rocks; that a *Fakīr* formerly took up his abode there, but having been eaten by a snake (an *ajgar*), one of enormous size, and an eater of human flesh, the people became alarmed; and no holy or unholy person has since taken up their residence on these rocky islands. Small boats fish under the rocks, and snakes, they say, abound upon them: when a gun is fired the echoes awaken and startle the myriads of birds that inhabit them. The proverb says, "The hypocrites of Bhagulpur, the *Thags* of Kuhulgaon (Colgong), and the bankrupts of Patna are famous."

SUNSET—A WILD SCENE.

The Ganges now presents an extraordinary picture, the expanse of water is very great, interspersed with low sand-banks; the sun is going down, and flocks of wild geese are passing to the other side the river. No human habitations are to be seen, nothing but the expanse of the broad river and its distant banks. After the heat of a day in India the coolness of the evening is most refreshing: the traveller quits his boats, and wanders on the banks of the Ganges, enjoying the wild, the strange beauty, and the quietude of the scene around him, until his attention is aroused by the yells of jackals, and the savage cry of pariah dogs, contesting with vultures, who shriek and flap their heavy wings, to scare the animals from their feast on some dead bullock. Beasts of the forest and birds of prey

"Hold o'er the dead their carnival:
Gorging and growling o'er carcase and limb,
They are too busy to look at him!"

they eye the traveller askance: they are too busy to look at him: but when the shades of evening fall, and the friends have left the dead, it may be the dying Hindū, on the banks of the river, trusting, that Ganga will receive him to eternal beatitude, then, in that solitary, that awful hour, the dying man may be awakened from his trance by the sharp tooth of the jackal, and the fierce beak of the vulture! Such is the power of superstition, that the Hindū might rejoice, even at this fearful moment, to end his days by the side of the sacred river, and escape the infamy of seeking refuge at the village of Chagdah.

"On Ganga's brink it is fearful to tread
By the fest'ring side of the tombless dead,
And see worms of the earth, and fowls of the air,
Beasts of the forest all gathering there;
All regarding man as their prey,
All rejoicing in his decay."

"Wheresoever the body is, thither will the eagles (or rather the vultures) be gathered together." (Luke xvii. 37.) The vulture is equally ravenous after dead bodies as the jackal; and it is very remarkable how suddenly these birds appear after the death of an animal in the open field, though a single one may not have been seen on the spot a long time before.

The jackal is considered an incarnation of Dūrga, when she carried the child Krishna over the Jumna, in his flight from King Kansa. The worshippers of the female deities adore the jackal as a form of this goddess, and present offerings to him daily. Every worshipper lays the offering on a clean place in his house, and calls the god to come and partake of it. As this is done at the hour when jackals leave their lurking places, one of these animals sometimes comes and eats the food. In temples dedicated to Dūrga and other deities, a stone image of the jackal is placed on a pedestal and daily worshipped. When a Hindū passes a jackal, he must bow to it; and if it passes on the left hand, it is a most lucky circumstance.

Crocodiles are very numerous in this part of the Ganges: they show themselves continually, swimming low in the water, peering over the edge of a sand-bank, or basking in the sun upon it. Near this place is a village full of a caste of people who live on the flesh of the crocodile; the *dāndīs* say they understand it smells rank and is very hard. In the evening you sometimes hear a shrill peculiar scream, which the men declare is the cry of the crocodile. When fired at, they slink quietly into the water. The long-nosed crocodile is not so formidable as the snub-nosed alligator: it is said the latter will attack men, the former avoids them if possible. Human bones and ornaments are sometimes found in the interior of these animals. To disagree with a superior, under whose command you may be, is, the natives assert, "To live in the river and be at enmity with the crocodile."

BENARES—RAJ GHĀT.

The appearance of Benares, from the Ganges, is very beautiful. It is covered with buildings to the water's edge: the architecture of some is Hindū, of others Muhammadan; many of them are of imposing appearance and great picturesque beauty. The magnificent flights of steps called *Ghāts,* which descend deep into the river, are thronged at all times with people; some fetching water, others washing, and most performing their ablutions in the sacred stream. The view is surprisingly picturesque, and so singular, that no city in Europe can convey an idea of Benares.

For a detailed account of Benares or *Bunarus,* deriving its name from two streams, the Burna and the Ussee, you may refer to a beautiful work by the late James Prinsep, Esq., who states that the ancient denomination of this city was *Kashi,* "The splendid," whereof the fabulous wonders are fully detailed in the *Kashi-Khund,* one of the chapters of the *Skundu-Poorana.* According to this mythological history, Kashi is a place of most profound antiquity, sanctity, and splendour: it has survived in age a hundred lives of Brahma, each of whose days is equal to 4,320,000,000 of years; it stands raised from the ground, supported upon the *trisūl* or trident of Mahadēo, and is never shaken by earthquakes: the whole city was once of pure gold, but has since degenerated into stone and brick.

Bunarus (Sanscrit, *Bàrànusee*) quasi *Burna-Ussee,* or from Raja Bunar, who founded the town A.D. 1000. It contains about 600,000 souls—one-fourth Musalmans. The city stands on a high ridge of *kankar* (nodules of lime stone), free from the floods which sometimes cover all its suburbs. The houses are of stone, from two to six stories high, with terraces on the summit, and open interior courts. The streets are very narrow, from four and a half to nine feet wide, with low doors on each side. The trade is in sugar, cotton, indigo, opium, *kimkhwab,* jewels, &c.

No building in the town now standing can be traced to a higher antiquity than the time of Man Singh, who was Rāja of Jypoor in the reign of Akbar. Both the temple and the *man mundil,* or observatory, described by Tavernier, were erected by him. The astronomical instruments were not added until the time of Jy Singh, 1680, more than a century later.

The scene now before you on the left bank of the Ganges represents the holy city commencing from Raj Ghāt, the place at which the steamers from Calcutta are moored, as well as pinnaces and budjerows. The distance from the latter place via the Bhagirathī is 696 miles, and by land or *dāk*, 428. The civil and military station is about four miles inland. Native merchants bring goods of all descriptions for sale to the steamers and vessels anchored off this ghāt; jewellery, shawls, portraits of the natives, &c. Provisions of all sorts, with wine and beer, are procurable in the city.

The house situated above Raj Ghāt is the hotel that was so recently destroyed, when the fleet of magazine boats containing gunpowder was blown up, the vessels having been moored off this ghāt.

Bruhma Ghāt is ancient, and of irregular form; it derives its name from a temple of Siva, under the title of Brumeswur, "the Lord of Brumha." The temple and ghāt were repaired (perhaps built) 200 years ago, by the Marhattas, and again recently by the ex-Peshwa Baji Rāo. From the number of Marhatta families residing in the neighbourhood, and the comparative privacy of the spot, it is by courtesy set apart as a bathing-place for their women. They resort hither in groups, with their children and female servants. Their wet garments are shifted with dexterity under a large wrapper, which is also worn over their silk dresses, in passing through the streets. The Brahman of the ghāt is of course a privileged person; he receives a small gratuity for taking care of the clothes, and brass or silver water vessels; he also affixes the *tiluk* (frontal mark) and pronounces the *muntra* or morning benediction upon his spiritual daughters.

On this ghāt wood is collected in large piles for sale: "Our wood is sold to us." (Lamentations v. 4.) The poor Hindū, living in the country never purchases wood for fuel. When such a person removes to a large town, he speaks of it as a great hardship, that he is obliged to buy his very fire-wood.

Benares is considered as the most holy city of India, and it is certainly one of the most picturesque. "A little to eat and to live at Bunarus" is the wish of a pious Hindū; but a residence at this place is rather dangerous to any one inclined to violate the laws.

"Kala-Bhoirāva the Tremendous, is a naked Siva, smeared with ashes; having three eyes, riding on a dog, holding in one hand a horn, and in another a drum. In several places in Bengal this image is daily worshipped. Siva, under this name, is regent of Kāshī (Bunarus). All persons dying at Bunarus are entitled to a place in Siva's heaven; but if any one violate the laws of the shastrŭ during his residence there, Kalŭ-Bhoirŭvŭ after death grinds him between two millstones."

The dog carries Kalŭ-Bhoirŭvŭ, a form of Siva, and therefore receives the worship of many Hindūs, whenever his master is worshipped; still he is considered as an unclean animal: every offering which he approaches is considered unacceptable to the gods, and every one who touches him must purify himself by bathing.

THE MINARETS.

THE MINARETS.

The Madhoray Ghāt and *musjid* or mosque, are now before you—the mosque was erected by Aurunzebe, on the site and with the materials of the temple of Vishnū. The mosque has little architectural beauty to boast of, but the *minars* have been deservedly admired for their simplicity and boldness of execution. They are only eight and a half feet in diameter at the base, and the breadth decreases to seven and a half feet, while they have an altitude of 147 feet 2 inches, from the terraced floor of the *musjid* to the *kalsā* or pinnacle. The terrace is elevated about eighty feet above the river at low water level.

The musjid and the minars were repaired by Mr. James Prinsep—a hazardous undertaking as regarded the latter, for they were both found to incline outwards fifteen inches from the perpendicular. One of them was struck by lightning the very day the scaffolding was removed, but it escaped with the displacement of a stone in the upper cornice. Several instances have occurred of men throwing themselves from the top of the southern minaret. One of them, a man who had gambled away his money and his wife during the *Diwâlī*:—another, a sailor, who was killed on the spot:—another, a *Fakīr*, who, falling through the tiles and mat-work of a roof, scraping the flesh from his sides, alighted on the floor beneath, with every bone safe. Such an escape was deemed miraculous; and crowds attended to minister to one so favoured by heaven. The *Fakīr* disappeared immediately on recovering from his bruises, and sundry solid moveables of his host disappeared with him.

Men, women, and children bathe together, uniting the worship of the Ganges or of the gods with their ablutions, washing their long hair with mud, making clay images for *pūjā*, (worship), or pouring out libations to their deceased ancestors, whilst the children gambol in the water, or collect clay to assist in making the great image of Bhīm Singh the giant, which is so frequently seen on the side of a ghāt, or that of Hunumān the monkey god. The Hindūs pour out water to the sun, three times a day; and to the moon at the time of worshipping her, which illustrates a passage in Scripture, "To pour out drink-offerings to the queen of heaven." (Jer. xliv. 17.)

Ghoosla Ghāt unites great solidity with a graceful and appropriate elevation: the double-arched door case in front of the gate has a very rich effect under the strong shadows of midday, giving an artificial magnitude to the entrance, in just proportion to the dimensions of the front. The river rises above the top of the doorway, entering the staircase, and affording a comfortable bath within, where there are convenient recesses on the sides of the steps for the accommodation of bathers.

The ferry-boat is crossing the river laden with camels, buffaloes, and cows.

RAJRAJESWURREE GHĀT.

On the sands in the foreground is the hut of a *Baniyā*, or grain merchant, from whom the *dandīs* procure *chabenī*, the parched grain of Indian corn (maize), also flour for their *chappatīs*. A group of pilgrims are seated on one side of the hut.

Rajrajeswurree Ghāt, which is seen in the distance, takes its name from an ancient temple of *Devī,* under the appellation of *Rajrajeswurree* ("queen of queens"). The title *Devī,* is usually applied to Bhawanī. The façade of this building is a good specimen of the mixed style of Hindū and Moresque architecture; the former is observable in the lower half of the central compartment; while the projecting stone gallery, with its parapet, *tukya mootukka,* and the domed octagonal *buruj* at the two corners, giving relief to the rectangular pavilion in the centre, are seen to be essentially Moorish, from the character of the pillar, and scalloped arch (*mehrab*).

The man in green is one of a very fine corps of men, called Gardner's Horse; they were raised by the late Colonel Win. Linnæus Gardner, a most highly distinguished and gallant officer: they are such masters of their horses and weapons, that it is said, single-handed, nothing can resist them; and one of these men, well known in the up-country, was considered to be the finest horseman in India. For an account of Colonel Gardner's romantic, adventurous, and distinguished life, we refer you to a work lately published, the "Wanderings of a Pilgrim during Four and Twenty Years in the East."

The two men who next appear belong to Skinner's Horse, a most efficient irregular corps, taking its name from its gallant colonel, by whom it was raised and stationed at Delhi. Skinner's Horse rendered important services in the Mahratta and Pindaree campaigns. They are well mounted and appointed, and are an intelligent, fine body of men: with a lance of great length, they are exceedingly expert, and excellent shots with the matchlock, a most unwieldy fire-arm.

A native carriage, called a *bilī,* drawn by two bullocks, stands in the rear: these decorated carriages are principally used by women in the higher ranks of life; and within the curtains, which are closely drawn and fastened down, a lady is completely protected from the profane gaze of man.

In the distance you now behold the Dusaswumed Ghāt. The mythological legends which give rise to the name of this ghāt and temple, are connected with the story of Divadas's usurpation of Siva's kingly authority in *Kashī.* Siva having sent from heaven the *yoginis,* or heavenly nymphs, and tried various other stratagems in vain, to turn the earthly monarch aside from virtue, next deputed Brumha himself, who entered the place, disguised as an old Brahman, and obtaining access to the king, received permission from him to perform ten (*dus*) *aswumedha,* or horse sacrifices, upon the spot here represented. The horse sacrifice, as described in the *purans,* is a very curious ceremony. A horse having peculiar colours and qualities is selected, and after a course of *pūja* (worship), is turned loose upon the world, followed by the sacrificing party, with an armed retinue: if stopped by the sovereign of another country through which the animal may pass, war must be declared, and the interrupter of the sacrifice subdued:—in this way, after traversing the world, the horse returns, and is put to death by suffocation.

THE SNAKE CHARMERS.

The group of natives seated on the ground are a particular cast of Hindūs, who profess to charm serpents, to reduce them to subjection, and to prevent their poison from proving fatal. They roam about the country, carrying a boa constrictor in a basket, which they twine around their necks and display to the passers by. They have also a number of the cobra di capello, which, being placed on the ground, rear themselves up, and, spreading out their hoods, sway themselves about in a fashion which the men call dancing, accompanied by the noise of a little hand-drum. The snake charmers strike the reptiles with their hands, and the snakes bite them repeatedly on their hands as well as on their arms, bringing blood at every bite: although the venomous fangs have been carefully removed, the bite itself must be disagreeable; nevertheless the natives appear not to mind it in the least. At the conclusion of the *tamāshā* (fun), they catch the cobras and cram them all into *gharās* (earthen vessels), and carry the boas off in a basket. The snake charmers remind us of the text, "They are like the deaf adder, that stoppeth her ear; which will not hearken to the voice of charmers, charming never so wisely." (Psalm lviii. 4, 5.)

The two men on the left are pilgrims with holy water. In the cold season of the year, Hindūs from all parts of Upper India, perform pilgrimages to the sacred places on the Ganges: although the stream throughout is considered holy, there are parts of peculiar sanctity, such as Hurdwar, Benares, Allahabad, &c. The roads swarm with devotees; they proceed in large groups, generally well dressed, carrying on their shoulders a large bamboo, supporting at each end a covered basket, containing small stumpy bottles of the thinnest green glass, having long necks: they are filled with Ganges water at the sacred places, and sealed with the seal of the Brahman. These people travel all over the country, selling the sacred water at a high price at the distant stations. Some of the bottles contain a quart; others are not above two inches high; they are of all sizes, and the price varies accordingly. The salutation of these people on passing is, "*Ram ram,*" or "*Bom bom Mahadēo,*"—a pilgrim of this class is called a *Kanwar-wālā*. The men come for this water to place it in their houses for religious and medicinal uses, and sometimes perform a journey on the occasion of five or six months; it is also used in the English courts of justice, in administering an oath to an Hindū. The frames in which the baskets are carried are decorated with feathers of the sacred peacock and small red flags; and every party appears to have one amongst them more ornamented than the rest, with a large arched cover, and numerous bells attached to it.

A *jumna-pār* goat, so called because these goats are bred on the other side the Junma, is lying on the ground—they are of enormous size, with very broad, long, thin, and silky ears, as soft as velvet. These animals are better adapted for marching than the small Bengalī goat; but unless they can go into the *jangal* and browse, they become thin and lose their milk.

On the opposite side of the river is the Jellinghy flat and her steamer, returning from Allahabad to Calcutta. The steamer herself is not the vessel in which passengers live; but attached to, and towed by her, is a vessel as large as the steamer herself, called a flat, built expressly to convey passengers and government treasure. It is divided into cabins, with one large cabin in the centre, in which the passengers dine together. The deck is covered with an awning.

The view on the left of the native vessel exemplifies the structure of the ghāts on the water's edge. The continuity of the line of steps is interrupted by hundreds of stone piers of various forms, which may be classed under three distinct heads: some are merely intended to give solidity to the masonry; others are built for the accommodation of the *ghātiyās* (ghāt attendants), and *gangā-putras* (sons of the Ganges), who enjoy hereditary possession of most of the ground between high and low water mark, and whose ancestors have resided on the spot from time immemorial in hereditary attendance upon pilgrims; the third sort consists of *mut'hs* or small temples, erected at the expense of pilgrims and others: they generally have a flat roof, which serves the *ghātiyā* as a *chabūtāra* or terrace to sit and converse upon. The large *chatrs*, or umbrellas, so numerous on the ghāts, are fixtures, to protect the people from the intense heat of the sun in India.

On the river's edge are seen one or two *murhīs*—chambers into which the sick are removed when at the point of death, that their sins, to the last moment of existence, may be washed away by the holy stream.

In the midst of hundreds and hundreds of temples and ghāts, piled one above another on the high cliff, or rising out of the Ganges, the mind is perfectly bewildered: it turns from beauty to beauty, anxious to preserve the memory of each; and the sketcher throws down the pencil in despair. Each ghāt presents a study: the intricate architecture, the elaborate workmanship, the elegance and lightness of form, and the picturesque groups of natives that crowd to their devotions, form as fine a subject for a picture as an artist could select.

How soon Benares, or rather the glory of Benares—its picturesque beauty—will be no more! Since the year 1836 many ghāts and temples have sunk, undermined by the rapid stream which now sets full upon the most beautiful cluster of the temples on its banks: some have been engulphed, some are falling; and ere long, if the Ganges encroach at an equal rate, but little will remain of the glory of the most holy of the Hindū cities.

In the rains, some of the temples are submerged to the cornice; many Hindūs, notwithstanding, are bold enough to swim through an impetuous current, and to dive under the porch and doorway, for the honour of continuing their customary worship despite of perils and personal inconvenience.

JULSYN GHĀT.

Julsyn *Ghāt* and Raj Bulubh Shīwala are now before you. On the terrace of the latter is a brahmanī bull: these animals walk about the buildings with seeming indifference, ascending the steps, mixing with the crowd, and constantly attending for their food. They are seldom disturbed; but when molested they are vicious, and will use their horns. The rice and flowers offered to the idols are swept up, and for the greater part eaten by the brahmanī bulls. The proverb says:—"At Benares you should be on guard against the women, the sacred bulls, the steps, and the devotees."

The principal Hindū temples in Benares are crowded with people of both sexes and of all ages, who daily assemble to pay their devotions to the deity of the place, from the hour of eight in the morning until nearly four in the afternoon. The form of worship is very simple: the votary enters the temple and prostrates himself, praying aloud; he then rises and strikes a bell suspended over a form of *Mahadēo,* thrice repeating the word *bom,* or hail, at each stroke; then putting a few grains of boiled rice, and a small quantity of milk or oil, or Ganges water, on the Mahadēo, he strews a few flowers over it, and, repeating the same, sometimes adorns the head of the idol with a chaplet of flowers. This ceremony being over, the votary lays down a few cowries, and retires to make room for others. The women generally enter with their garments quite wet, after having performed their ablutions in the Ganges. The quantity of milk, oil, water, and flowers, thrown about the place, renders it dirty and wet until the evening, when, the crowd retiring, the Brahmans clean the temple for the next day.

The music and bells of a hundred temples strike the ear amidst the buzz of human voices; at the same time the eye rests on the vivid colours of different groups of male and female bathers, with their sparkling brass vessels, or follows the holy bulls as they wander in the crowds munching the chaplets of flowers liberally presented to them. Then, as night steals on, the scene changes, and the twinkling of lamps along the water's edge, and the funeral fires and white curling smoke, and the stone buildings lit up by the moon, present features of variety and blended images of animation, which it is out of the artist's power to embody.

The large building that now appears is on Oomraogir's *pushta* or *ghāt*. On the exterior of the building is a *mut'h,* an Hindu temple, dedicated to Ganesh, the god of wisdom, and the patron of literature. In *pūja* this idol is invoked ere any other god is worshipped. Ere a pious Hindū commence any sort of writing he makes the sign of Ganesh at the top of the page. With the simplicity of the child he unites the wisdom of the elephant: his writing is beautiful, "Behold! he writes like Ganesh!" Who can say more? He is called two mothered, uniting the elephant's head to his natural body, therefore having a second mother in the elephant. The worshippers pour oil and the holy Ganges water over the head of this god, who is thus bathed daily; and offerings of boiled rice and flowers are made at the time of prayer. Around the idol are placed the vessels used in *pūja,* brass bells, the conch shell, the holy spoons, flowers, &c. In the Museum is a solid white marble image of Ganesh, which weighs 3¼ cwt. For a further account of this idol, see the frontispiece, and the Introduction to the "Wanderings of a Pilgrim during Four and Twenty Years in the East."

The Fākir seated on the ghāt is one in the highest stage of exaltation, in which clothing is almost dispensed with, and his only *garment* is a *chatr,* an umbrella made of basket work: his long hair and his beard, matted with cow-dung and ashes, hang in stiff straight locks to his waist, his body is smeared with ashes; he always remains on the same spot, and when suffering from illness, a bit of tattered blanket is thrown over him. Passers by throw cowries and grains of boiled rice at his feet, he remains speechless, disregards all visible objects, asks for nothing, but subsists on alms. He will not answer any question addressed to him, which elucidates the proverb: "Talking to a man in ecstasy (of a religious nature) is like beating curds with a pestle." Persons in this state affirm that their minds do not wander after worldly things, that they live in a state of pleasure, abstraction, and joy, and that they have attained to that state of perfection required by the *shastrs.*

His red flag is displayed from a bamboo, below which is a small lantern made of coloured *ubruk* or talc; sometimes the lamp is formed of clay, pierced through with fret-work in remarkably pretty patterns. The Hindūs suspend lamps in the air on bamboos in honour of the gods during a particular month, and in obedience to the *shastrs*. The offering of lamps to particular gods is an act of merit, so this offering to all the gods, during the auspicious month, is supposed to secure many benefits to the giver. Lamps suspended from bamboos are also indicative of the ceremony in honour of Ananta, the great serpent.

On another bamboo is displayed the *trisūl* or trident of Mahadēo, and a small double-headed hand-drum, shaped like an hour-glass, called *damaru*, used by *Fakīrs*; and in front by the side of the Devotee, is an altar, or pillar, hollowed at the top, containing the sacred *tulsī* plant (ocimum sanctum) purple stalked basil. This plant is worshipped in honour of a religious female who requested Vishnu to allow her to become his wife. Lukshmī, the goddess of beauty, and wife of Vishnu, cursed the woman on account of the pious request she had preferred to her lord, and changed her into a *tulsī* plant. Vishnu, in consideration of the religious austerities long practised by the enamoured devotee, made her a promise that he would assume the form of the *shalgram*, and always continue with her. If one of these sacred plants die, it is committed in due form to *Ganga-jee*: and when a person is brought to die by the side of the sacred river, a branch of the *tulsī*, the shrub-goddess, is planted near the dying man's head, and the marks upon the *shalgram* are shown to him. This pebble god is a small heavy black circular stone, rather flattened on one side, with the *cornu ammonis* strongly marked upon it. Devotees walk round the sacred plant, pour water upon it, and make *salām*. Of an evening a little *chirāgh*, a small lamp, is burned before it. In the courts of justice the Hindū swears by the Ganges water on which is placed a branch of the *tulsī*.

MANIKURNĪKA GHĀT.

A brahmanī bull is going up to the idol Ganesh, expecting a share of the flowers that are offered to the image. In the distance a band of pilgrims are coming down to fill their baskets with holy water; and in the foreground is a picturesque figure, also a carrier of holy water, which is put into small sealed bottles placed in baskets suspended from a bamboo poised on his shoulder, over which is a covering of red cloth.

A tank of peculiar sanctity is now before you, on the steps of which men are ascending and descending: it is called the *Chakra kunda*, and its history is as follows:—"After one of the periodical destructions and renovations of the world, Siva and his bride were alone in the *ananda-vana*, or happy forest, occupying the present site of Munikarniká, they found, as man and wife may sometimes do, that their tête á tête was growing dull, and to vary the party, Siva created Vishnu. After a while, the married pair wished again for privacy and withdrew into the forest, desiring Vishnu to amuse himself by doing what was fit and proper; which, after some consideration, he judged to be a supply of water for the irrigation of the trees, and with his *chakra*, or discus, he dug a hole, which he filled with the ambrosial perspiration from his body, induced by his hard work; and the pool so dug and filled, has remained a spot of peculiar sanctity, termed, from the *chakra*, or discus, *chakra kunda*, or *chakra puskkarnī*, discus-pond. When Siva returned and saw what Vishnu had done, he nodded his head in approbation so energetically, that the jewel (*mani*) of one of his ear-rings (*karniká*) fell off, and the place was thenceforth called *Manikarnika*." (See *Kasi Khand*, Part I. chap. 26).

A Brahman sitting beneath a porch is reading aloud, with his book on his knees, and bending his body backwards and forwards as he reads.

Beneath the shade of a fine *pīpal* tree (ficus religiosa) is a four-headed and holy piece of sculpture, with the bull (*nandī*) reposing before it; also another singularly sculptured stone representing two heads, their bodies formed of snakes entwined. The *pīpal* is universally sacred: the Hindūs are seen in the early morning putting flowers in *pūja* at the foot of the tree, and pouring water on its roots. They worship the idols placed beneath it in a similar manner, and they believe that a god resides in every leaf, who delights in the music of their rustling, and their tremulous motion.

Near this place is the spot on which the dead are burned; it is dedicated to Vishnu, as *Jalsāī*, or "sleeper on the waters;" and there, many a Hindu widow has devoted herself to the flames with the corpse of her husband. In the Museum is a brazen image of *Jalsāī* floating on Anantā, the great serpent.

THE HINDŪ SCHOOL.

In the Bengalī schools a boy learns his letters by writing them, never by pronouncing the alphabet, as in Europe; he first writes them on the ground with a stick, or his fingers; next with an iron style, or a reed, on a palm-leaf; and next on a green plantain-leaf. The Bengalī schoolmasters punish with a cane, or a rod made of the branch of a tree; sometimes a truant is compelled to stand on one leg, holding up a brick in each hand, or to have his arms stretched out, until he is completely tired. Almost all the villages contain common schools. The allowance to the schoolmasters is very small: for the first year's education, about a penny a month, and a day's provisions; when a boy writes on the palm-leaf, twopence a month; after this, as the boy advances in learning, as much as fourpence or eightpence a month is given. There are no schools for girls among the Hindūs. "Jesus stooped down, and with his finger wrote upon the ground." (John viii. 6). Schools for children are frequently held under trees in Bengal, and the children who are beginning to learn, write the letters of the alphabet in the dust. This saves pens, ink, and paper. "The sin of Judah is written with a pen of iron." (Jeremiah xvii. 1). The letters are formed by making incisions on the palm-leaf: these books are very durable.

The scene now represents the *gyan-bapī*, or the well of knowledge, which is regarded as peculiarly sacred by the Hindūs, and it is related that it was dug by Isana with his *trisūl*, or trident, when he was wandering about Kashī. One of the officiating Brahmans is seen receiving the offerings of rice, &c. from a party of pilgrims, just about to commence the circuit of the temples. If a rich Hindū present any thing to an inferior, the latter, as a mark of respect, puts it on his head. An offering of cloth, for instance, received at a temple, the receiver not only places on his head, but binds it there. The rice and flowers were formerly thrown into the well; but they rendered the water so putrid, that a defence of planks has been since put up to prevent it. The man near the *gyan-bapī* carrying a staff, is a *dŭndī fakīr*. This name is given because these devotees receive a staff (*dŭndŭ*) when they first enter this order. The Brahmans, on meeting one, prostrate themselves before him. The *dŭndī* shaves his head and beard every four months. He travels with a staff in one hand, and an alms-dish in the other; he does not beg or cook his food, but is a guest at the houses of the Brahmans. The ceremonies to which this order attend, are, repeating the names of Vishnŭ, bathing once a day, and, with closed eyes, meditating on the attributes of the god by the side of the river. When about to bathe, they besmear themselves all over with the mud of the Ganges. The *dŭndīs* do not burn, but bury their dead, repeating certain forms of prayer.

THE BALANCING GOAT.

In front of a beautiful Muhammadan Mosque a group is assembled around an Hindostanī juggler, with his goat, two monkeys, and several bits of wood, made in the shape of an hour-glass. The first piece he places on the ground, the goat ascends it, and balances herself on the top: the man by degrees places another bit of wood on the edge of the former; the goat ascends and retains her balance: a third piece, in like manner, is placed on the top of the former two pieces; the goat ascends from the two former, a monkey is placed on her back, and she still preserves her balance. The man keeps time with a sort of musical instrument, which he holds in his right hand, and sings a wild song to aid the goat: without the song and the measured time, they say the goat could not perform the balance. A grass-cutter is looking on: he has just returned from cutting a bundle of *dūb*-grass: every horse in India has his *sāīs*, or groom, and his grass-cutter. When a beautiful *begam* (a native princess) is suffering from the pangs of jealousy, she often exclaims, "I wish I were married to a grass-cutter!" because a man of that class is too poor to be able to keep two wives.

The man on the right is a religious mendicant, a disciple of Siva. When this portrait was taken, his long black hair, matted with cow-dung, was twisted like a turban round his head: he was dreadfully lean, almost a skeleton. His left arm had been held erect so long, that the flesh had withered, and the skin clung round the bones most frightfully; the nails of the hand, which had been kept immoveably clenched, had pierced through the palm, and grew out at the back of the hand, like the long claws of a bird of prey. His skeleton arm was encircled by a twisted stick, the stem perhaps of a thick creeper, the end of which was cut into the shape of the head of the cobra di capello, with its hood displayed; and the twisted withy looked like the body of the reptile wreathed around his horrible arm. His only garment was the skin of a tiger, thrown over his shoulders, and a bit of rag and rope. He was of a dirty ashen colour from mud and paint; perhaps in imitation of Siva, who, when he appeared on earth as a naked mendicant of an ashy colour, was recognized as Mahadēo, the great god. This man was considered a very holy person. His right hand contained an empty gourd and a small rosary, and two long rosaries were around his neck of the rough beads called *mundrāsī*. Acts of severity towards the body, practised by religious mendicants, are not done as penances for sin, but as works of extraordinary merit, promising large rewards in a future state. The *Byragī* is not a penitent, but a proud ascetic.

A very small and beautifully-formed *ginī* (a dwarf cow) was with him. She was decorated with crimson cloth, embroidered with cowrie shells, and a plume of peacocks' feathers as a *jika,* rose from the top of her head. A brass bell was on her neck, and around her legs were anklets of the same metal. Many *Fakīrs* lead these little dwarf cows about the country, they are fat and sleek, and considered so holy that they will not sell them.

A barber sitting on a ghāt, is shaving an Hindū, he makes use of water, but not of soap, while he shaves all round the head, leaving a tuft of hair in the middle of the back of the head, which is commonly tied in a knot. Shaving is usually done under a small shed or a tree, very often in the street or road.

We have now given as many views of Benares as it is possible to introduce within the limits of our Diorama, and we take leave of the holy city with regret. The *Vedas* and *Shastrs* all testify that "Viswaswara is the first of *Devas, Kashī* (Benares) the first of cities, *Gangā* the first of rivers, and charity the first of virtues." Vishveshvur, "Lord of the Universe," is one of the most exalted titles of Siva.

THE FORTRESS OF CHUNAR.

The scene now represents Chunar, a fortress of considerable natural strength, situated on an insulated rock, about 150 feet high, forming the extremity of a low range of hills, on the right bank of the Ganges, about eighteen miles from Benares. In December, 1765, the Company's troops, commanded by Major Pemble, stormed the place, and were repulsed with severe loss. The defences were irregular, following the outline of the eminence on which they were erected: several heavy batteries were mounted on the ramparts; but the native garrison trusted more to the inaccessible nature of the approach, and to the facilities it possessed for rolling down stones upon any assailants,—of which missiles, a large supply was always held in readiness on the ramparts. The fortress was again invested, and on the 8th of February, 1765, the *Killadar* of the Fort surrendered the keys to Major Stibbert. It is an invalid station, although not reckoned a healthy spot, owing to the great heat arising from the stone: it completely commands the river, and is used as a place of confinement for state-prisoners. Snakes are numerous, and boys bring the cobra di capello for sale to boats. In the Magazine is a large black slab, on which the deity of the Fort is said to be ever present, with the exception of from daybreak until the hour of nine A.M., during which time he is at Benares. Tradition asserts, that the Fort would never have been taken by the English, but for the absence of their god Burtreenath.

A little above the Fort is a temple: tradition states it to contain a chest, which cannot be opened, unless the party opening it lose his hand—four thieves having so suffered once in an attempt upon it. It is also recorded, that the deified giant Bhīm Singh, built the fortress of Chunar in one day, and rendered it impregnable.

A native has just succeeded in crossing the river on a bundle of reeds; his clothes placed on the top of his head are safe from wet, and with one hand he paddles along. On the outskirts of the village is seen a remarkably ancient Banyan-tree, the Ficus Indica.

In front of the tomb of a *Pīr* (a Muhammadan saint), three followers of the prophet are at their devotions. A *Shāmiyāna,* or awning, screens the tomb from the sun and rain: the standards of Hussan and Hussein are displayed, and daily coloured lanterns are suspended from the top of high bamboos.

THE PERSIAN WHEEL.

A woman is sticking cakes of cow-dung on the wall to dry for fuel. This article, called *oplā,* is generally used by the poorer classes; 1280 cakes are sold for a rupee: when well prepared and dried it blazes like wood. On the right is a fine Persian wheel: the water is brought up in *gharas,* red earthen vessels fastened round its circumference; it is worked by two bullocks, and gives an abundant supply. A wheel of this sort is perhaps superior to any other method of drawing water.

MIRZAPŪR.

Mirzapūr is a military cantonment, famous for its beautiful ghāts, and noted for its carpet manufactory and cotton mart. Some remarkably picturesque Hindū temples are on the *ghāts,* with fine trees in the back ground. The cliff is abrupt, and the river is always crowded with vessels full of merchandise: steamers having plenty of cargo to land are generally detained here four or five hours. Mirzapūr is from Calcutta, *via* Bhagirathī, 748 miles, and by dāk route, 455.

The scene before you is very singular; it represents the finale of the *Kalī-pūjā* festival: the goddess is seen on a platform in the boat in the foreground, covered by an awning, and adorned with flags: on the steps of the *ghāt,* a similar image is being put into a boat, and from every part of the city the worshippers are bringing forth the idols. One of the boats is towed by a *dinghī,* in which they are firing a *feu de joie* from a matchlock.

In the house of the Bengalī *babū* you beheld a *nāch,* and the worship of the goddess Dūrga, a yellow woman, with ten arms. You have now before you another form of the same Hindū deity, under the name of Kalī, the black, the terrific. When this goddess is worshipped in the month of May, it is called the *Phuluharī* festival, on account of the quantity of fruits and flowers offered to the idol at this particular season: animals are sacrificed in her honour, and jack fruit and mangoes are presented to her in that particular month.

The day after the worship, the people carry the goddess in state to the river, and place the image on a platform, between two boats; the worshippers, attended by the discordant music of tom-toms (native drums) and horns, row the image out into the stream, and sink her in the deep waters: the women weep and utter lamentations on parting with the idol.

This goddess is represented as a black woman, with four arms: in one hand she carries a scimitar, one is bestowing a blessing, another forbids fear, and the fourth holds the head of the giant whom she slew.

She wears a necklace of skulls, her tongue hangs out of her mouth, her jet-black hair falls to her heels. Having drunk the blood of the giants she slew, her eyebrows are bloody, and the blood is falling in a stream down her breast: her eyes are red, like those of a drunkard: she stands trampling on her husband Siva. Kālī had a contest with the giant Ravŭna, which lasted ten years: having conquered him, she became mad with joy, and her dancing shook the earth to its centre. To restore the peace of the world, Siva, her husband, threw himself amongst the dead bodies at her feet. She continued her dancing, and trampled upon him. When she discovered her husband, she stood still, horror-struck and ashamed, and threw out her tongue to an uncommon length; by this means Siva stopped her frantic dancing, and saved the universe. "The Philistine cursed David by his gods." A Hindū sometimes in a fit of anger, says to his enemy, "The goddess Kalī shall devour thee; may Dūrga destroy thee!"

THE TIMBER RAFT.

The picturesque *ghāt* of Sirsya is in the distance, in front of which is an enormous boat, called a *Kutcher*, or *Kutchuā*; the bows and the stern are both square. A vessel of this description has frequently two rudders, like the one before you. It is laden with bales of cotton, which extend, supported on bamboos, far beyond each side of the boat. The next vessel is a large *patailī*, called a *ghor-daul*, or *ghora-wal*, because the bows are ornamented with a horse's head. She is laden with salt.

In the foreground is a timber raft, one of the most picturesque objects to be seen on the Ganges. The men who accompany the raft have a strangely wild appearance; fresh from the *jangal*, they come down with the floating timber for scarcely any payment, just enough to feed them. They are small in stature, their skins are very dark, they shave the head completely, and their bodies are all but naked. They direct the course of the raft with long bamboos; a small thatch is erected upon her, under which they creep, and there they sleep. A picture in itself is the wild, strange-looking timber raft, which is generally decorated with two or three small red flags, and is always accompanied by a very small, narrow canoe, hollowed out of the trunk of a tree.

ALLAHABAD.

The fortress of Allahabad was built by Akbar Shah in 1581. On the 11th February, 1765, the governor of the fort, Alī Beg Khan, surrendered it to the Company's troops, under the command of Major Fletcher, and marched out with his garrison, under safe conduct. Thus in one week Chunar and Allahabad, the two most important fortresses in Shuja-oo-Dowlah's possession, fell without loss into the hands of the English.

The fortress is erected upon a point of land, stretching out into the waters at the junction of the sacred rivers. One of the holiest places on the Ganges is pointed out by numerous flags at the spot where it joins the Jumna, just below the fort. The Saraswati is supposed to unite with them *underground*, whence the junction is called *Trivenī*, or *Tribenī*. This spot is so holy, that a person dying there is certain of immediate *moskh*, or beatitude, without risk of further transmigration. The blue waters of the Jumna contrast strongly at the junction with the muddy hue of the waters of the Ganges. On the sands below the fort, the *Bura Mela*, or great fair, is held annually; it lasts about two months, and attracts devotees and merchants from all parts of India. At that period, also, *lākhs* and *lākhs* of natives come to Prag; they make *pūja*, shave, give money to the *Fakīrs*, and bathe at the sacred junction. Suicide committed at the *Benī* is meritorious in persons of a certain caste, but a *sin* for a Brahman! The ancient city of Prag, acquired the name of Allahabad from the Musalmān conquerors of India.

The buildings occupied by Shah Allum when he resided in the fort, still retain traces of their former grandeur, and some of the apartments command a fine view of the Jumna that flows beneath. An enormous pillar, formerly prostrate near the gateway in the fort, has been set up on a pedestal, under the superintendence of the late Colonel Edward Smith. The natives call it *Bhīm Singh ké lāt*, that is, Bhīm Singh's walking-stick: some of the inscriptions on the *lāt* are in unknown characters—those of the mighty dead, who have disappeared from the earth, leaving records imperishable, but incomprehensible.

The steam vessels and tugs which navigate the Ganges from Calcutta terminate their voyage at Allahabad.

THE SATĪ.

The scene now before you represents a *Satī*, the burning of a Hindū widow with the corpse of her husband. The event here represented took place on the 7th November, 1828, near Raj ghāt, under the Mahratta *bund* (an embankment raised to prevent the encroachment of the Ganges). The woman was the wife of a rich *buniyā* (a corn-chandler), and she determined to burn on his funeral-pile. The magistrate sent for her, used every argument to dissuade her, and offered her money. Her only answer was, dashing her head against the floor, and saying, "If you will not let me burn with my husband, I will hang myself in your court of justice." If a widow touch either food or water from the time her husband expires until she ascend the pile, she cannot, by Hindū law, be burned with the body; therefore the magistrate kept the corpse *forty-eight* hours, in the hope that hunger would compel the woman to eat. Guards were set over her; but she never touched any thing. A procession of people accompanied the widow from her dwelling to the river-side; she walked in the midst, dressed in a red garment, and the corpse, placed on a charpaī, fixed on long bamboos, was carried on men's shoulders. About 5000 people were collected together on the banks of the Ganges: the pile was built, and the putrid body placed upon it.

After having bathed in the river, the widow lighted a brand, walked round the pile, set it on fire, and then mounted cheerfully: the flame caught and blazed up instantly; she sat down, placing the head of the corpse on her lap, and repeated several times the usual form, "*Ram, Ram, sātī; Ram, Ram, sātī;*" *i.e.* "God, God, I am chaste." As the wind drove the fierce fire upon her, she shook her arms and limbs as if in agony; at length she started up, and approached the side to escape.

An Hindū—one of the police who had been placed near the pile to see that she had fair play, and should not be burned by force—raised his sword to strike her, and the poor wretch shrank back into the flames. The magistrate seized and committed him to prison. The woman again approached the side of the blazing pile, sprang fairly out, and ran into the Ganges, which was within a few yards. When the crowd and the brothers of the dead man saw this, they called out, "Cut her down! knock her on the head with a bamboo! tie her hands and feet, and throw her in again!" They rushed down to execute their murderous intentions, when some English gentlemen and the police drove them back. The woman drank some water, and having extinguished the fire on her red garment, said she would mount the pile again and be burned. The magistrate placed his hand upon her shoulder (which rendered her impure), and said, "By your own law, having once quitted the pile, you cannot ascend again; I forbid it." He sent her in a palanquin, under a guard, to the hospital. The crowd made way, shrinking from her with signs of horror, but returned peacefully to their homes; the Hindūs annoyed at her escape, the Musalmāns, saying, "It was better that she should escape, but it was a pity we should have lost the *tamāshā* (amusement) of seeing her burnt to death." The woman said, "I have transmigrated six times, and have been burned six times with six different husbands; if I do not burn the seventh time, it will prove unlucky for me!" "What good will burning do you?" asked a bystander: she replied, "The women of my husband's family have all been *satīs*: why should I bring disgrace upon them? I shall go to heaven, and afterwards re-appear on earth, and be married to a very rich man."

The woman was about 25 years of age, and possessed some property: had she performed *satī*, her relatives would have raised a little cenotaph, or a mound of earth, by the side of the river; and every Hindū who passed the place returning from bathing, would have made *salām* to it—a high honour to the family. The *shastrs* say, "There is no greater virtue than a chaste woman burning herself with her husband." Mothers collect the cowries, strewn by a satī as she walks round the pile, ere she fires it, and hang them round the necks of their sick children, as a cure for disease.

The woman became an outcast: her own and her husband's family would lose caste, if they were to speak to her; no Hindū will eat with her, enter her house, or give her assistance; and when she appears, they will point at her, and give her abuse. Many years after this event took place, the woman regained caste by giving large feasts and donations to the Brahmans.

In the Museum are five *kalsas*, or crowns of unglazed pottery, some of which formerly decorated the *satī* mounds in Alopee Bagh, near Allahabad, and the rest were brought from Ghazipūr. There are also two black stones, apparently very ancient, on which figures are carved, brought from the *satī* mound of the widow of a Brahman, at Barrah.

About two years after this event at Allahabad, the practice of *satī* was abolished, by order of government.

THE SATĪ.

The fine building here represented is a *dhrum-sala,* or place to distribute alms, at Benī Māhadēo Ghāt; it is dedicated to a form of Māhadēo, which stands in the *shiwālā,* or little temple above. Under the arches in the lower part, by the side of the Ganges, is an enormous figure of Ganesh; the worshippers pour oil and Ganges water over the image, with rice and flowers, and hang chaplets of flowers around its neck: the idol is generally dripping with oil. The red flag, at the end of a long bamboo displayed from the *pīpul* tree, denotes the residence of a *Fakīr*. The temple is very picturesque, and the foliage adds to the beauty of the scene.

SULTAN KHUSRŪ'S MAUSOLEUM.

The *sarā'e,* or caravansary, at Allahabad, built by Sultan Khusrū, is a noble one, and the gateway through which you pass to the *bāghīcha,* or garden bearing his name, is very fine. The garden is a large space of ground, enclosed by a high wall, containing three tombs and a *baithakhāna,* or pavilion. These palace-like tombs, amongst which is that of Sultan Khusrū's, are splendid mausoleums. Tho first and largest monument is that of the Sultan, in which he is buried; it is a handsome building, and within it is deposited a beautifully-illuminated kurān. Sultan Khusrū married a daughter of the Wuzeer Azim Khan; he was the son of Jehāngīr, and his mother was the daughter of the Rajpūt Prince Bagwandas, of Amber. The other monuments are those of Noorjahān and the Jodh Bā'ī; the fourth building is a pavilion, in which visitors are allowed to live for a short time, during a visit to the garden. Around the tombs are some of the finest and most beautiful tamarind-trees. These trees, called by the natives *imlī,* are generally found around or sheltering the tombs of revered or sacred characters. The natives are impressed with a notion that it is dangerous to sleep under the tamarind-tree, especially during the night.

Just beyond the gates of the *sarā'e,* is a *bāolī,* a magnificent well, with underground apartments; it is a most remarkable and curious place, and the well is a noble one.

A company of pilgrims, carriers of holy water, are *en route* to the junction, to fill their bottles at the *benī,* or bathing-place. They are passing some of the tombs of the faithful.

In the foreground are some aloes. In India the hedges are full of this plant, and it flowers annually.

THE GRAM GRINDER.

In front of a native village a woman is spinning, and on the right is another Hindū woman, a gram grinder. Gram (*chāna, cicer arietinum,* chick pea) is used for the food of horses in India. It is ground in a *chakkī,* or mill, which is formed of two flat circular stones, the lower of which is generally fixed in the earth, and from its centre a peg passes through a hole in the upper stone, and forms a pivot on which the upper stone works. The gram is put in through this hole in the upper stone, and the flour works out at the edges between the two stones. When there is much work to be done, two women will sit on the ground and grind the same mill, which is placed between their legs. This is the sort of mill spoken of in Scripture:

"Two women were grinding at the mill, the one shall be taken and the other left." Matt. xxiv. 41.

HURDWAR.

Two children are playing with some meal in a basket; one of them is adorned with a number of charms, fastened on a string. The *ta'wīz,* or charm, is an armlet, to ward off evil spirits, and all misfortune. The native beds, resting against the wall on the right, serve as beds by night, and as resting-places by day.

HURDWAR.

Hurdwar, on the right bank of the Ganges, a place of great sanctity, is celebrated as the resort of Hindū pilgrims, in amazing numbers. Hurdwar, or *Hurīdwar,* (the gate of Hurī, or Vishnū,) is also called *Gangū-dwāra*—as at this place the Ganges, having traversed 150 miles from its secluded mountain birth-place, and having forced a passage through the last barrier or gate (*dwāra*), emerges in a broad clear stream upon the plains. Hurdwar contains many fine buildings parallel with the course of the river, some of which have their foundations in the sacred waters. They are generally of brick, but many are of very fine white freestone. The bed of the river is intersected with low woody islands, and is a full mile broad in the rainy season.

A fair takes place annually at Hurdwar, in the month of April, lasting nearly a fortnight; that being the period chosen by pilgrims, who flock from all parts of India to perform their ablutions in the Ganges: it is held in the bed of the river, which at that period is nearly dry. Two or three hundred thousand people are attracted to this fair, and every twelfth year, it is supposed a million of people assemble at this place. The scene is interesting in the highest degree. Merchants from Calcutta meet with others from Osbeck Tartary, and Cabul; and thousands of Seiks attend the fair. Horse merchants from Bokhara and Cabul occupy the central parts of the dry bed of the river; those from Tūrkistān encamp at the back of the town. Elephant dealers traverse the roads of the fair with their animals, morning and evening; and the place is crowded with camels, mules, and shawl and jewel merchants; in fact, merchandise of every description is collected at the fair from every part of the Eastern world, and it is difficult to convey even a faint idea of the swarms of living creatures, men and beasts of every description, which occupy every foot of ground during the fair.

The Hindūs receive from the Brahmans a certificate of having performed the pilgrimage; and carriers of holy water attend in great numbers to bring away the sacred stream in bottles, carefully sealed and stamped.

THE BATHING GHĀT.

The principal bathing ghāt has been lately rebuilt in a most splendid manner by the Government of Bengal, under the superintendence of an officer of engineers; it is now both elegant and commodious, and will prevent the destruction of so many human beings, which so often occurred by the sudden rush of the devotees through the old and narrow ghāt to reach the water at the propitious moment, which was often at midnight. The auspicious moment is calculated by the Brahmans, who aver that a great increase in the efficacy of the rite is derivable from its performance, when Jupiter is in Aquarius, which happens every twelfth year, or when the sun enters Aries.

SIMLA—THE CONICAL HILL.

A wandering mendicant in the foreground is playing on an *ektara*, a one-stringed instrument, formed of a gourd, surmounted by peacocks' feathers—the Paganini of the East!

BARH.

The scene before you represents the encampment of the Commander-in-chief at Barh, at the foot of the hills, distant about thirty miles from Simla. Here the baggage elephants, and camels, deposit their loads, a part of which are carried up the mountains by the hill men; the remainder, with the carriages, palanquins, and tents, are either sent back to the plains, or placed in *godowns* belonging to a Simla firm at Barh. The ladies of the party are sitting in *jampāns*, ready to ascend "The Hills," as these mountains are called, from being at the foot of the Himalaya. The *jampān* is a sort of arm-chair, with a top and curtains to it, to afford shelter from the sun or rain; long poles are affixed to it, and it is carried by four *Paharīs*, singular-looking little black, hill fellows, harnessed between the poles after their fashion. A group of them are sitting near the *jampāns*. They are little fellows, with flat ugly faces, like the Tartar race, dressed in black woollen coarse trowsers, a blanket of the same over their shoulders, and a rope round their waists; a black greasy round leather cap on their heads, sometimes decorated all round the face with bunches of freshly gathered hill flowers. They are very honest, and very idle; moreover, most exceedingly dirty. The women are good-looking and strong. Polyandry is a common institution. Gentlemen ascend the hills either in a *jampān* or on a *gūnth*, a hill-poncy, a most sure-footed, sagacious animal, who will carry you safely round the most dangerous places, where you have a wall of rock on the one side, and a precipice on the other. A *jumna-par* goat, with its long silky ears, is lying on the ground near a shawl goat from Cashmere. Some men of a corps of irregular horse are in attendance on the Commander-in-Chief, and the *tom-tom wālā*, with his drum, is seated on his blanket, on which the people throw cowries, and sometimes *paisā*, small copper coins: a *tom-tom wālā* is a constant attendant on every camp.

SIMLA—THE CONICAL HILL.

The view now before you represents the conical hill at Simla; it was taken by Lieutenant-Colonel Luard from his house, called The Craigs. Simla is about 7000 feet above the level of the sea; it is not many miles from Rampore, the chief town in the valley of the Sutledge, and is one of the favourite places of resort of Europeans during the hot season.

As the chosen retreat of Governors-General and Commanders-in-Chief, from the burning plains of India, the place has enjoyed for some years past many considerable advantages. A great number of residences have been built on the hills; the roads are good; there is a church, a school, an observatory, an amateur theatre, &c. You have a glimpse of the snowy ranges in the distance. The conical hill is crowned by Stirling Castle; and the house below it was then inhabited by Colonel Birch, the Judge Advocate General. The flag-staff points out the residence of his Excellency the Commander-in-Chief, and the houses below, on the left, are those occupied by the Aid-de-camps. Two hill men are in the foreground, with the baskets in which they carry provisions on their backs.

GANGOUTRĪ.

SIMLA.

The view is a continuation of Simla; and one of the residences now before you is that of Mr. Gubbins, of the Bengal Civil Service.

The hills are covered with the finest vegetation, and the views are beautiful. The evergreen oak flourishes in magnificence, the deodar fir rises to enormous height, and the bright crimson-flowered rhododendron is a *forest tree*, not a shrub, as you have it in England. Violets are under every rock, the wild notes of the hill birds are heard in every direction, and health, strength, and spirits are imparted by the pure, delicious, and bracing mountain air.

FAGOO.

On the Hill of Fagoo, here represented, is a Traveller's Bungalow, constructed of wood. A group of *Paharīs*, or hill men, are on the right, and in the distance are the snowy ranges of the Himalaya. Water is procured from the *khuds*, as the deep narrow valleys between the hills are called, where it is found in little rills.

THE GANGES.

This mountainous and picturesque scene represents the force with which the holy river rushes downwards from the deep recesses in the mountains, until it passes the last barrier of rocks, and emerges on the plains near Hurdwar.

The *dēodar*, Pinus dēodara, rises to a magnificent height in these regions, sometimes measuring 100 feet: its oil, called *dēodar*, is used by the natives as a powerful remedy in rheumatic attacks. Leopards and bears inhabit the forests, and the musk deer is sometimes, though but rarely found. The black and the golden eagles of the Himalaya swoop over the precipices, and a great variety of remarkably beautiful pheasants are found here. Specimens of all these birds may be seen in the Museum.

THE SNOWY REGIONS.

As you approach Gangoutrī, you enter on the snowy regions; and in the scene before you, the hill men, with baskets of provisions, are toiling up the steep ascent, for which their stout and sinewy limbs are well adapted; and pilgrims are ascending the mountain. An English gentleman, seated beneath a small tent, is resting, refreshing himself, and enjoying the warmth of the fire his attendants have kindled, ere he re-commences the toilsome ascent of the snowy mountains.

GANGOUTRĪ.

Gangoutrī, the source of the most sacred river in Hindostan, is now before you. The pious Hindū believes, that in this awful solitude Mahadēo sits enthroned in clouds and mist, amid rocks that defy the approach of living thing, and snows that make desolation more awful. Surrounded by gigantic peaks entirely cased in snow, and almost beyond the regions of animal and vegetable life, an awful silence prevails, except when broken by the thundering peals of falling avalanches. Cold, wild, and stupendous, the dazzling brilliancy of the snow is rendered more striking by its contrast with the dark blue colour of the sky; and at night the stars shine with a lustre they have not in a denser atmosphere. Gangoutrī (*Gangā avatārī*), marked 10,319 feet above the sea, is the celebrated place of pilgrimage, near to which the Ganges issues: its course has not been traced beyond Gangoutrī; for the stream, a little farther, is entirely concealed under a glacier or iceberg, and is supposed to be inaccessible. The *mandap*, or Hindū temple, built by a Ghoorka chief, is of stone, and contains small statues of Bhāgīrath, Gangā, and other local deities. It stands on a piece of rock about twenty feet higher than the bed of the Ganges; and at a little distance there is a rough wooden building to shelter travellers. The last day of his journey the pilgrim fasts, and on his arrival at the sacred spot, he has his whole body shaved; after which he bathes, performs funeral obsequies in honour of his deceased ancestors, and makes presents to the Brahmans.

To perish by cold in the mountains during a pilgrimage, forms one of the methods by which the Hindūs may meritoriously put a period to their existence; it is also one of the Hindū atonements for great offences. The pilgrim must remain seven days at Gangoutrī: when he is about to return, he obtains some of the offerings which have been presented to the idol or idols, and brings them home to give to his friends; these consist of sweet-meats, *tulsī* leaves, the ashes of cow-dung, &c. To obtain its full benefit, the pilgrimage must be performed on foot. A trifle is paid to the Brahman for the privilege of taking the water, which the Hindūs believe is so pure as neither to evaporate nor become corrupted by being kept and transported to distant places. Notwithstanding the great efficacy attributed to this pilgrimage, Gangoutrī is but little frequented, owing to the hardships to be endured, and the great difficulties that are met with on the route; the accomplishment of it is supposed to redeem the performer from many troubles in this world, and ensure a happy transit through all the stages of transmigration he may have to undergo.

The snowy peaks of Gangoutrī rise in glittering whiteness high above the clouds. Look on those mountains of eternal snow,—the rose tints linger on them, the white clouds roll below, and their peaks are sharply set upon a sky of the brightest, clearest, and deepest blue. Who may describe the solitary loveliness, the speaking quietude that wraps these forest scenes? Who can look unmoved on the coronets of snow that crown the eternal Himalaya?

"Our fathers worshipped in this mountain." (John iv. 20.) In these awful solitudes, where eternity is throned in "icy halls of cold sublimity," the Hindūs think "men ought to worship." The pilgrim gazes with delight on the aërial mountains that pour down Gangā and Yamunā from their snow-formed caves, and enjoys those solemn feelings of natural piety with which the spirit of solitude imbues the soul.

We have now traced the course of the Ganges, from the branch called the Hoogly, which flows past Fort William, Bengal, to Gangoutrī, its source in the Himalaya. The Diorama is concluded, and we trust that satisfaction and pleasure have been experienced by the audience who have accompanied us on the pilgrimage.

THE MUSEUM.

is open for the inspection of those who have honoured with their presence the Diorama of Hindostan.

THE END.

9 789358 007633

Printed by Libri Plureos GmbH in Hamburg,
Germany